How to Really Know the Will of God

How to Really Know the Will of God
Richard L. Strauss

LIVING STUDIES
Tyndale House Publishers, Inc.
Wheaton, Illinois

BIBLE TRANSLATIONS

From J. B. Phillips: *The New Testament in Modern English*, Revised Edition, © J.B. Phillips 1958, 1960, 1972. Used by permission of Macmillan Publishing Co., Inc.

From *The Modern Language Bible*, The New Berkeley Version, © 1959, 1969 by Zondervan Publishing House.

From the *Amplified New Testament*, © The Lockman Foundation 1954, 1958. Used by permission.

From *New International Version*, Copyright © New York International Bible Society, 1973. Used by permission.

From *The Living Bible*, © 1971 Tyndale House Publishers. Used by permission.

How to Really Know the Will of God
was originally published under the title
Decisions! Decisions!

First printing, Living Studies edition, July 1982
Library of Congress Catalog Card Number 81-86692
ISBN 0-8423-1537-3, paper
Copyright © 1979 by Richard L. Strauss
All rights reserved
Printed in the United States of America

To my mother and dad,
who taught me from my earliest days
to do the will of God

CONTENTS

Part One God's Perfect Plan 11
  1 The Game Plan 13
  2 All Your Ways 22
  3 He Will Be Our Guide 30
  4 One Step at a Time 38

Part Two Your Personal Preparation 47
  5 Knowing the Shepherd 49
  6 Not My Will 57
  7 The Renewed Mind 67

Part Three God's Primary Provision 77
  8 Equipped for the Journey 79
  9 This Is the Will of God 86
  10 Charting the Course 96
  11 But I Felt Led 105

Part Four Other Practical Principles 113
  12 Ask God 115
  13 Flashing Lights and Clanging Bells 124
  14 Use Your Head 134
  15 Peace Like a River 144
  16 Right Where You Are 154

THE TIME IS NOW

Every child of God faces decisions. Rarely do we get through an entire day without being confronted with many different choices—most of them minor, some of them major. Is there any guarantee that we can consistently do the right thing?

Not many people get interested in the subject of divine guidance until they face a decision of supreme importance. By then it may be too late. We prepare ourselves to handle the big decisions of life by dealing properly with the small ones. So the way to prepare for the major crossroads of the future is to begin learning in the present. The time to think about this subject is now.

And God has help available. His Word is filled with practical suggestions for making proper choices. This book is an attempt to bring that information together for your encouragement and assistance. In the words of the prophet Isaiah, "This is the way, walk ye in it" (Isaiah 30:21).

PART ONE
GOD'S PERFECT PLAN

CHAPTER 1
THE GAME PLAN

The management experts tell us we need to plan our lives. "Set goals for yourself," they say. "Decide where you want to be and what you want to be doing one year from now, five years from now, ten years from now. Map out a plan for getting there from where you are, and begin to follow that plan faithfully."

They even suggest that our plan should reach right down to our daily schedules, that the things we do today should be contributing toward the fulfillment of our ultimate goals. Each day, they say, we should make a list of the things we want to accomplish in order of their priority, then work our way through the list. "Plan your work and work your plan" is the catchy little phrase they use to encourage us. And the solemn warning is sure to follow: "To fail to plan is to plan to fail."

Most of us want to be successful in what we do. We enjoy the respect that goes with success and the sense of satisfaction that accompanies accomplishment. So we may listen to the experts, lay out a plan for our lives, follow that plan precisely, and still fail. Why? Because for the child of God there is another factor to consider: God also has a plan for our lives.

The truest kind of success from God's perspective can be attained only when we follow his plan rather than our own

We may reach every goal we ever set for ourselves, and we may earn the admiration of all our friends and the respect of all our associates, and still feel a sickening emptiness inside if we have ignored God's plan.

You see, God saved us to know and to do *his* will. In a message to a recent convert named Saul of Tarsus, Ananias declared, "The God of our fathers has chosen you to know his will and to see the Righteous One and to hear words from his mouth. You will be his witness to all men of what you have seen and heard."[1] Paul was chosen by God to come into an understanding of his will and to carry it out. He lived his whole life with awareness that God had a plan for him to follow.

That awareness made an immeasurable difference. Some twenty-five years after his conversion, in the face of great affliction, Paul confidently affirmed, "But none of these things move me, neither count I my life dear unto myself, so that I might finish my course with joy, and the ministry, which I have received of the Lord Jesus, to testify the gospel of the grace of God."[2] The word "course" was used of the race course laid out for a runner to follow in the Olympic Games, the plan for the race which was prepared ahead of time by the judges. Paul's great aspiration was to follow God's course for his life.

And he did it. At the end of his life he reflected back over his years as a believer and said, "I have fought a good fight, I have finished my course."[3] And he used the very same word he had used years earlier. He was writing, this time, from death row in a Roman dungeon. He was soon to be martyred for his faith. Yet his life was a success; he had fullness of joy and a satisfying sense of accomplishment because he had completed the course God had laid out for him. He had done the will of God.

Some will say, "Wait a minute; that was the great Apostle Paul. Sure, God had a plan for *his* life, but what's that got to do with *mine?*" All right, here it is straight. God has a plan

---

[1] Acts 22:14, 15 (NIV)
[2] Acts 20:24 (KJV)
[3] 2 Timothy 4:7 (KJV)

for your life, too. Unless you are convinced that he does, you will probably lay your own plans and choose your own way. And someday you may look back and say, "Well, here I am, right where I wanted to be. But why do I feel so hollow and unfulfilled?"

So we must firmly establish this basic biblical concept before we go any further: *God has a plan for your life.*

TOO GOOD TO BE TRUE?

Nowhere is the principle more lucidly stated than in this pivotal verse: "For we are His workmanship, created in Christ Jesus for good works, which God prepared beforehand, that we should walk in them."[4] There is no doubt about how we got saved. We are God's workmanship; we were created anew in Christ Jesus by the regenerating work of his Spirit.[5] He did it all of his own grace. "For by grace you have been saved through faith; and that not of yourselves, it is the gift of God; not as a result of works, that no one should boast."[6] But there was one very important reason why God re-created us in Christ Jesus. It was so we might *do good works.*

"So what?" you say. "Everyone should do good works, shouldn't he? Why is that so special?"

The special thing about the good works God wants each of us personally to do, is that they were selected ahead of time by him. They were "prepared beforehand," that is, they were planned by God before we were even born. And now our responsibility is to accomplish those specific good works which God laid out for us so long ago.

When a football coach prepares for a big game, he lays out what he calls a game plan, a strategy for that particular contest. Before the game begins he knows exactly what he wants his players to do and how he wants them to respond in certain situations. They can choose other strategies, but the coach usually finds that they perform best when they follow

---

[4]Ephesians 2:10 (NASB)
[5]Cf. 2 Corinthians 5:17; Titus 3:5
[6]Ephesians 2:8, 9 (NASB)

the game plan he has prepared beforehand. Just so, there are many plans we can choose for our lives, many different directions we can go. But only one plan will provide the opportunities to do all the good things the divine Coach wants us to accomplish.

Only one road will bring us in touch with all the people he wants us to meet and influence for him. Only one direction will include all the circumstances he wants to use to mold and enrich our lives. We function best when we stick to his game plan, when we walk the path he has mapped out for us and do the things he has planned for us in advance.

Some Christians are convinced that they are too small and unimportant for God to be that interested in them. "People like the Apostle Paul, yes. But me? Never!" Do you not realize what God is saying in this passage? Each one of us is so important to him that he actually charted a course for each life before we were ever born. To think that he cares for us that much is almost too good to be true. And it is not an isolated fact found only in this passage of Scripture. Look at some others.

David said, "You saw me before I was born and scheduled each day of my life before I began to breathe. Every day was recorded in your Book!"[7] The context assures us that while we were still in our mothers' wombs, God was watching over us, superintending our development.[8] But more exciting still is that he had already sketched out all our days for us. Before we ever saw our first light, he had designed the direction he wanted our lives to take and the events he wanted to fill our days.

Look at it again in another notable Psalm. "The steps of a man are established by the Lord;/And He delights in his way."[9] The course which the believer's life should take is fixed or settled by God. And what joy it brings to God's heart when we follow the plan he has arranged for us. He delights in our way. Can there be any more doubt in your mind? God has a plan for every believer. He has a plan for you.

[7] Psalm 139:16 (TLB)
[8] Cf. Psalm 139:13-15
[9] Psalm 37:23 (NASB)

A PARADE OF WITNESSES

These simple statements of fact are enough to convince us, but there is still further evidence. God gives us an impressive array of living illustrations to cement this truth in our souls. Every reference in Scripture to a person doing the will of God reaffirms the fact that God actually did have a will for him, a plan for him to follow. There are many such examples in the Bible, as we shall see in the chapters to come. Look at just a few extraordinary ones here.

The first is Isaiah. While there is no doubt that the Servant of Jehovah in Isaiah's prophecy refers to the Lord Jesus Christ, Isaiah was probably speaking from his own experience as well when he said: "Listen to me, all of you in far-off lands: The Lord called me before my birth. From within the womb he called me by my name . . . the Lord who formed me from my mother's womb to serve him, who commissioned me to restore to him his people Israel, who has given me the strength to perform his task and honored me for doing it!"[10]

God brought Isaiah into being in order to fulfill a particular task. He formed him in his mother's womb for the purpose of performing a unique and urgent mission, that of calling Israel back to himself. And he assured Isaiah that he would supply him with the needed resources to do the job. God had a plan for Isaiah's life.

Another great prophet comes into view. Listen to God's encouraging word to Jeremiah. "Before I formed you in the womb I knew you,/And before you were born I consecrated you;/I have appointed you a prophet to the nations."[11] Jeremiah balked at first. "Alas, Lord God! Behold, I do not know how to speak,/Because I am a youth."[12]

We sometimes do the same thing when we first learn about God's plan for us. "Who, me, Lord? Certainly you must have the wrong person. I can't do that." But God is there with the answer. "Do not say, 'I am a youth,'/Because everywhere I send you, you shall go,/And all that I command you, you shall speak./Do not be afraid of them,/For I am with

[10]Isaiah 49:1, 5 (TLB)
[11]Jeremiah 1:5 (NASB)
[12]Jeremiah 1:6 (NASB)

you to deliver you . . . Behold, I have put My words in your mouth./See, I have appointed you this day over the nations and over the kingdoms,/To pluck up and to break down,/To destroy and to overthrow,/To build and to plant."[13]

Many times Jeremiah must have thought back to the day he first learned about God's plan for his life. The people to whom he preached taunted him, rejected his message, spread false rumors about him, threw him into prison, and broke his tender heart with their rebelliousness and sin. Jeremiah's persecutors are seldom mentioned anymore. Few of us remember their names even after reading them in the inspired account. But Jeremiah's name lives on with honor because he followed God's plan for his life.

Let's go back to the Apostle Paul for a moment. We saw that God saved him to do his will, but there is further evidence that God had laid out the course for his life even before he was born. Here is how he explained it: "But when He who had set me apart, even from my mother's womb, and called me through His grace, was pleased to reveal His Son in me, that I might preach Him among the Gentiles, I did not immediately consult with flesh and blood."[14]

Before Paul drew his first breath, God had already planned for him to pioneer the proclamation of the gospel to the Gentile world. That sense of divine mission gave him confidence and courage throughout his Christian life and ministry. In five of his epistles he introduced himself as an apostle of Jesus Christ *by the will of God.*[15] He knew he was doing exactly what God wanted him to do. He was fulfilling God's plan for his life.

How can we talk about life plans without mentioning the earthly life of God's Son? The Father's plan for Jesus' life was clearly settled from the foundation of the world,[16] and the details of the plan fill the volumes of the Old Testament. On one occasion Jesus said, "All things that are written by the prophets concerning the Son of man shall be accomplished."[17] They had to be accomplished. They were part of

---

[13]Jeremiah 1:7-10 (NASB)
[14]Galatians 1:15, 16 (NASB)
[15]Cf. 1 Corinthians; 2 Corinthians; Ephesians; Colossians; 2 Timothy
[16]Cf. Revelation 13:8
[17]Luke 18:31 (KJV)

19 The Game Plan

the Father's plan, and Christ came to do the Father's will. He confidently declared, "For I have come down from heaven not to do my will but to do the will of him who sent me."[18] Doing the Father's will was his greatest joy and delight. It was more important to him than eating.

Do you remember that episode at Jacob's well in Sychar? The disciples had just returned from the city with provisions, and they were urging their tired and hungry Master to eat. "I have food to eat that you know nothing about," he said to them.[19] When they questioned him further, he clarified his statement. "My food . . . is to do the will of him who sent me and to finish his work."[20]

To finish his Father's work, to follow his Father's plan, to fulfill his Father's purposes—that was Christ's highest goal. The writer to the Hebrews expressed the Savior's sentiments like this: "Then I said, 'Here I am—it is written about me in the scroll—I have come to do your will, O God.' "[21]

But again, we're talking about prophets and apostles, and above all, about the Son of God himself. Aren't there any little people to illustrate the point—inconspicuous folks like us?

How about an obscure, unnamed, unknown beggar who couldn't even see? If God had a plan for his life, would you feel more like God might be interested enough in you to have a plan for your life? This particular man was born blind, and the religious leaders of his day always blamed such misfortunes on sin. So when Jesus and his disciples saw him, the disciples asked, "Rabbi, who sinned, this man, or his parents, that he should be born blind?"[22]

Here is Jesus' answer: "It was neither that this man sinned, nor his parents; but it was in order that the works of God might be displayed in him."[23] God had allowed that man to experience all those years of blindness so that at this precise moment in time he might not only give him his physical sight, but also remove the scales of spiritual blind-

---

[18]John 6:38 (NIV); cf. also John 5:30
[19]John 4:32 (NIV)
[20]John 4:34 (NIV)
[21]Hebrews 10:7 (NIV)
[22]John 9:2 (NASB)
[23]John 9:3 (NASB)

ness from his soul and provide an unanswerable testimony to others about the person and power of Jesus Christ. It was part of God's plan for his life. And after he had experienced the joy of knowing Christ and the freedom of having his sins forgiven, I doubt that he ever regretted those years of blindness.

THERE'S NOBODY JUST LIKE YOU

If God had a plan for that blind beggar, he certainly has one for you. And I can assure you that his plan is custom made to fit you personally. Nobody else has one just like it. And since it was made for you, it is the very best plan you can possibly follow.

You see, God never made another human being just like you. You are unique and distinct in all of his creation. And since he made you, he is the only one who knows you perfectly and completely. He knows you better than you know yourself. Therefore, he is the only one who can intelligently formulate a plan for your life that will utilize all of your potential to its optimum advantage.

God knows your abilities and he knows your weaknesses. "O Lord, you have examined my heart and know everything about me."[24] He knows that some of the things you think are your strengths may really be limitations, and some of the things you think are liabilities are the very things which he can use with great power. Just as he made you, he also constructed a plan that is tailored to your personality and abilities. His plan has to be better than anything you could ever devise. In fact, his plan is perfect. That is exactly what the Apostle Paul calls it: "that good, and acceptable, and *perfect* will of God."[25]

He not only knows *you*; he also knows the *future*. Most of us want our lives to go well, and we know that the decisions we make will have something to do with that. We also want things to go well for the ones we dearly love, and we know that our decisions will also affect them. So we lay our plans and make our choices on the basis of what we think will be

[24]Psalm 139:1 (TLB)
[25]Romans 12:2 (KJV)

21 The Game Plan

best for all concerned. But unfortunately we do not always know what will be best because we do not know the future. As Jeremiah put it, "O Lord, I know it is not within the power of man to map his life and plan his course."[26]

We really do not know how things are going to turn out ultimately. But God does. He knows us and he knows all the possible consequences of every alternative we can choose. So it makes no sense to choose any plan but his. That is the only one we know will turn out right.

If you were traveling through a dense and dangerous jungle and had no knowledge of where you were nor what the next step would hold, you would be foolish to run off from your guide and try to blaze your own trail. He knows the way. He can lead you to safety. It is even more foolish for any of us to try to make our own path through life. Our Divine Guide knows the way. Following his plan will bring success and satisfaction to us and great glory to him.

[26] Jeremiah 10:23 (TLB)

CHAPTER 2
ALL YOUR WAYS

Decisions, decisions—life is filled with decisions. And few things are more frustrating than the daily barrage of inconsequential questions that require a decision. They start as soon as you pry your eyes open and plant your feet on the floor in the morning. What clothes will you put on? What will you prepare for breakfast? Should you pack lunches for the kids or give them money to buy their lunches? (You don't like the hassle of packing them and you don't have enough money to buy them every day).

Should you drive the car to work or take the bus? If you drive, should you offer to take your neighbor with you or should you drive alone? (You need the car pool money but you don't like to waste the time and fight the extra traffic involved in dropping him off and picking him up again after work). Should you accept that invitation to dinner for tomorrow night—the one you've been waiting for so long—or should you go to the open house at your child's school?

And young people are not immune from the struggle of daily decisions. Jack is trying to decide whether to invite Jeannie or Joannie to the big banquet. Jeannie is wondering whether to accept Jack's invitation or wait for a better one. Soon the decisions get more difficult. Should you date each other again and start getting serious? Could you be meant for each other for life? Should you plan to marry at all?

Then there's the matter of education. What courses shall you take in high school? Shall you plan to go to college? If so, where? What should be your major? What vocation should you prepare for? How will you find a job? Where will you live? What about the possibility of a Christian service career? Some of the most momentous decisions in life are made by the time we reach our early twenties.

Then just when we think everything is settled and all our major decisions are over for awhile, suddenly we are faced with things like the purchase of a new house, or the possibility of a different job, or a major relocation to another part of the country, or the biggest business deal of our lives, or the question of having another child.

Wouldn't it be nice to have someone with us all the time who knew the right thing to do in every situation and who would tell us how to decide? Well, we do! He doesn't whisper in our ear and say, "Don't buy that car; it's a piece of junk," nor does he shout, "Join that church; it's the best in town." But he is there, and he does care about every detail of our lives, and he is willing to give us advice about anything we want to know.

WHO'S IN CHARGE HERE?

Nearly everybody is looking for guidance of some kind, and there are many places to turn for help in this old world. There are horoscopes, fortune tellers, palm readers, and spiritist mediums—all of which the Scriptures unequivocably condemn.[1] There are also professional counseling centers and guidance clinics of every shade and description, some of which are helpful and some of which are not.

It's good to know that our primary source of guidance as Christians is the God who not only knows the future but can do something about it. In fact, the Scripture says that we live in his world. He made it, he holds it together, he's in charge of it, he's interested in everything about it, and he controls every circumstance in it.

The Apostle Paul gave us a profound insight into this

---

[1]Deuteronomy 18:9-12; Isaiah 8:19; Galatians 5:20

magnificent truth about God when he referred to him as the one "who worketh all things after the counsel of his own will."² Two words in this verse help us understand the subject of God's will. The first is counsel (*boulē*). This *boulē* involves a careful deliberation leading to a firm plan and purpose. Nobody can thwart God's counsel, his sovereign design or decree. Because he is God, he cannot ultimately be defeated. And Paul says that God is continually working every detail in his universe toward the eventual accomplishment of his invincible plan. He will use every happening in fulfilling his purposes.³ Those purposes are unchangeable⁴ and irresistible.⁵ For example, God shall surely defeat Satan, destroy sin, establish his righteous rule on earth, and be glorified in his redeemed ones throughout eternity. Nothing can stop him.

But Paul said God's counsel is derived from his will. He calls it "the counsel of his own *will*" (*thelēma*), a more general word referring to God's wants, his wishes, his desires. *Thelēma* is the most common word for God's will in the New Testament. It is important to understand that it involves not his determinative decisions, as the previous word did, but his desires for us, what he wishes for us. When we speak of God's will or God's plan for our lives we are normally alluding to what he *wants* us to do, not what he has *decided* we will do. "God's plan" may mean his counsel, his irresistible decisions, his ultimate program; but it can also refer to his desires for us, and that is the way we are using "God's plan" in this book.

While God will work every event in time toward the ultimate fulfillment of his purposes, and while everything he decides to do grows out of his wishes, he does not necessarily bring to pass everything he desires. He does not force his wants and wishes on us, nor does he violate the volition he created in us.

For instance, God would like everybody to be saved. That is his desire, his will. He said so.⁶ But he will not coerce

---

²Ephesians 1:11 (KJV)
³Cf. Psalm 76:10
⁴Cf. Hebrews 6:17
⁵Cf. Romans 9:19; *Boulēma*, a related word translated "will" in KJV.
⁶Cf. 1 Timothy 2:4; 2 Peter 3:9

everyone to accept his gracious offer of forgiveness and life. Many will refuse it to their own eternal destruction.[7]

Furthermore, God would like all believers to carry out his wishes for their lives, to find and follow his plan for them, and he sometimes seems to arrange our circumstances in such a manner as to help us want to do his will. But he never forces it on us. It's still our decision to make. We can thwart his will if we so desire.

And because so many believers and unbelievers alike are resisting God's will and rejecting his plan, there is a great deal of needless pain and suffering in the world. We endure not only the consequences of our own rebelliousness, but often also the widespread results of the sins of other individuals and of nations.

Yet through it all this one remarkable truth stands unshaken: God will use "all things"—every circumstance whether happy or heart-rending, every detail of every person's life, every move of every nation on earth, every sin as well as every act of obedience, absolutely everything—to accomplish his own ultimate purposes. Our God is in charge of everything.

SO WHAT COLOR SOCKS SHALL I WEAR?

If God is the God of "all things," then it follows logically that he cares about everything in our lives. In other words, his plan for us includes every detail of daily living. That's a revolutionary concept to some people and it usually stirs up some lively debate. "Do you mean to tell me that God cares about what color socks I put on in the morning?" That is exactly what I mean. But wait just a minute! Please don't throw this book down in disgust yet. Hear me out. And begin by looking at the Word of God. The evidence is overwhelming.

"The Lord will guard your going out and your coming in from this time forth and forever."[8] God is interested in things as small and insignificant as when we go out and when we come in, and he is watching over us in either case. As one

---

[7]Cf. Matthew 7:13; Revelation 20:15
[8]Psalm 121:8 (NASB)

thought-provoking Psalm says, "O Lord, you have examined my heart and know everything about me. You know when I sit or stand. When far away you know my every thought. You chart the path ahead of me, and tell me where to stop and rest. Every moment, you know where I am. You know what I am going to say before I even say it. You both precede and follow me, and place your hand of blessing on my head."[9]

God cares about when we sit down and when we stand up, and that isn't one of the more momentous issues of life, is it? When we take a walk he is right beside us each step of the way, and he even cares about where we stop to rest and every word we speak. Job said that he even counts our steps.[10] The prophet Isaiah put it like this: "And the Lord will guide you *continually*."[11] His direction is available all the time and for everything.

Listen to the Lord Jesus: "Are not two sparrows sold for a penny? Yet not one of them will fall to the ground apart from the will of your Father. And even the very hairs of your head are all numbered. So don't be afraid; you are worth more than many sparrows."[12]

If God cares about little two-for-a-penny sparrows, he certainly cares about every detail in our lives. His care is so exact that it includes a running count of the number of hairs on our heads. Now that may be a very grave issue to the fellow who has only two or three left, but for most folks it would fall into the same general category as the color of their socks, or what they're going to cook for dinner, or when they're going to find time to wash the car. You see, God is interested in everything.

The Apostle Paul adds his inspired testimony. "And we know that all things work together for good to them that love God, to them who are the called according to his purpose."[13] Paul takes for granted that we know this, but I find that many Christians don't. They are convinced that some circumstances in their lives are out of God's control, that he doesn't care about their predicament, if he even knows about

[9]Psalm 139:1-5 (TLB)
[10]Job 31:4
[11]Isaiah 58:11 (TLB)
[12]Matthew 10:29-31 (NIV)
[13]Romans 8:28 (KJV)

27 All Your Ways

it at all. That God will work it all out for good seems to be the farthest thing from their minds. But he can, and he will, and that goes for "all things"—every particular in our lives.

"All right, I'm convinced," you say. "I believe God is interested in every detail of my life. Now does that mean that I have to worry about which pair of socks he wants me to put on in the morning?"

No, certainly not. That would be oppression and bondage. God doesn't want us to worry about anything, much less something so insignificant. He wants us to live in the joyous freedom of his Holy Spirit. Wondering whether we have carried out God's plan in every trivial non-moral matter could drive us to a padded cell, and unfortunately some folks have taken that route to emotional disaster. God allows us the privilege of expressing our own preferences in matters like that. He is pleased to include this freedom of choice in his plan for us.

What then are the implications of the all-inclusiveness of God's plan?

THE OPEN DOOR POLICY

Let's allow Solomon to explain it in what probably ranks as the all-time favorite passage on the will of God. "Trust in the Lord with all your heart, and lean not on your own understanding; in all your ways acknowledge Him, and He will direct your paths."[14]

Look again at those six words in the middle of the promise: "In all your ways acknowledge Him." We sometimes skip over that part so hurriedly that we miss its true import. To acknowledge him is literally to take notice of him, to consider him, to be conscious of his presence, to be aware that he is right there with us.

And how often are we to recognize God's nearness? In all our ways, in every activity of life, large or small. God wants us to consider him all the time, in everything. It isn't a matter of wondering or worrying about what he wants us to do. It's simply being constantly cognizant that the eternal God of the universe lives in our bodies through his indwelling Spirit,

---

[14] Proverbs 3:5, 6 (Berkeley)

that he is interested in every detail of our lives, and that he wants to control us completely. From that point on, the guidance is guaranteed. He promises that he will direct our paths.

Suppose you really can't make up your mind about a decision as trifling as the clothes you put on in the morning. What should you do about it? I would suggest that you mention it to your Friend—the one who is with you all the time, who cares about everything in your life, who has promised to give you advice about anything you need to know.

Now here's where I get more raised eyebrows. "Do you mean I should bother God about silly little things like socks?" That's exactly what the Apostle Paul told us to do. "Be anxious for nothing, but in everything by prayer and supplication with thanksgiving let your requests be made known to God. And the peace of God which surpasses all comprehension, shall guard your hearts and your minds in Christ Jesus."[15] Talk to him about it and he will give you a settled inner peace.

Notice again, please, how many things God invites us to talk over with him. Everything! God has an open door policy. Because he wants us not to worry about all those little decisions, he makes himself available to us all the time. He's ready to listen and help us with the smallest matters. And he's always on the job. He doesn't even take time out to sleep.[16] He wants us to cultivate the habit of taking all of our problems to him anytime we please.

Just in case you are still a little doubtful, Peter added this inspired testimony: "Cast *all* your anxiety on him because he cares for you."[17]

Many Christians seem to think that God is interested only in the big issues of life such as marriage, vocation, and geographical location. They run to God for guidance whenever they face a crucial decision at a major crossroads in their lives, but ignore him the rest of the time.

We may miss some of the most exciting events in God's plan for our lives unless we develop a new way of life, a new

[15] Philippians 4:6, 7 (NASB)
[16] Cf. Psalm 121:4
[17] 1 Peter 5:7 (NIV)

mind-set that says, "Lord, I acknowledge that you are with me and interested in everything I do. How do you want me to live today? Guide every step I take."

Listen to Paul's fervent prayer for the Colossians. "For this reason, since the day we heard about you, we have not stopped praying for you and asking God to fill you with the knowledge of his will through all spiritual wisdom and understanding. And we pray this in order that you may live a life worthy of the Lord and may please him in every way: bearing fruit in every good work, growing in the knowledge of God."[18]

That prayer can be answered in our lives as well as in theirs. We can please God *in every way*. Every minute detail can be exactly what he desires. Acknowledge him in everything. Share everything with him. Let him be a part of all you do. If we hope to find God's direction in the critical choices of life, we need to acknowledge him now in the commonplace.

[18]Colossians 1:9, 10 (NIV)

CHAPTER 3
HE WILL BE OUR GUIDE

Sheep are peculiar animals—timid, defenseless, and not necessarily known for their great intelligence. In fact, they are rather stupid. They don't know where to go, they don't know what is best for them, and they wander off absent-mindedly, getting themselves into dangerous situations. I read about one entire flock of sheep that stumbled absent-mindedly into a ravine, stacking one on top of the other, smothering themselves to death. Sheep obviously need a shepherd to lead them.

Isn't it interesting that God likens his people to sheep?[1] It isn't very flattering, but it is so very true. We do not always know what is best for us. Left to our own wisdom we inevitably get ourselves into trouble. We need a shepherd to guide us, and we need to know exactly what he wants us to do.

This is the point at which some Christians drop out of the game. They believe God has a plan for their lives and they may even agree that his plan includes every detail of daily living, but they are not convinced that he can or will communicate his plan to them. They may have groped in the darkness so long that they think God has purposely hidden his will from them. Or that his will is a deep, dark secret which only some special class of super-Christians can find.

[1] E.g., Psalm 100:3; John 10:27

Maybe because we talk about *finding* God's will they get the idea that it is lost or hidden, or that God is playing some kind of heavenly hide-and-seek game.

God's plan for our lives is much too important for that kind of foolishness. He does not take pleasure in making things difficult for us. He wants to show us his will far more than we want to know it. If we have not yet discovered what it is, it has to be our fault, not his. Finding God's will is not a matter of frantically searching for something hidden. It is following the divine Shepherd, and there is nothing mysterious about that.

Failure to follow him would be just plain stupid. That's what the Apostle Paul told the Ephesians. "So then do not be foolish, but understand what the will of the Lord is."[2] Failure to comprehend God's plan for our lives is *foolish*, a word that means literally "without the mind." Or, as we would say today, ignorant, stupid, dumb.

If God is going to call us names like that for not knowing his will, then he certainly must be trying to reveal it to us. We are driven to the indisputable conclusion that we *can* know God's plan for our lives. So let's look at some of the evidence.

A REPUTATION AT STAKE

First look at the ever-popular Shepherd Psalm.

> *The Lord is my shepherd,*
> *I shall not want.*
> *He makes me lie down in green pastures;*
> *He leads me beside quiet waters.*
> *He restores my soul;*
> *He guides me in the paths of righteousness*
> *For His name's sake.*[3]

Twice in those inspired verses the poet points to the divine Shepherd's definite direction. First, "He leads me beside quiet waters"—literally, "waters of rest." The hillsides of life may be rocky, treacherous, barren, fruitless. But our

[2]Ephesians 5:17 (NASB)
[3]Psalm 23:1-3 (NASB)

Shepherd knows where to find shady green resting places beside cool, refreshing brooks, and we can count on him to lead us to them when he knows we need them.

Second, "He guides us in paths of righteousness for His name's sake." "Paths of righteousness" may mean either "right paths" or "righteous paths." Whichever, the reason he guides us is for his name's sake. His name corresponds to his character, his reputation.

An ancient shepherd had to build himself a reputation for being trustworthy and dependable. If he were to lead a flock of sheep down the wrong path and get them lost, or lead them near a pack of wolves and get them killed, no sheep owners would ever entrust their sheep to him again. He did his job well for the sake of his reputation. God has maintained an impeccable reputation for faithfully guiding his people, and he isn't about to ruin it now. We can count on his willingness to make his plan known to us. His character requires it.

Can you picture a human shepherd, whose livelihood depends on the welfare of those sheep, trying to run off and hide from them or trying to get them lost? That's ridiculous! How can we think less of the divine Shepherd? Consider another analogy. Can you imagine a human parent, who has certain expectations of his children, refusing to tell them what he wants from them? That would be absurd. How can we think less of our heavenly Father? Jesus said, "If you, then, though you are evil, know how to give good gifts to your children, how much more will your Father in heaven give good gifts to those who ask him!"[4] We have a right to expect the good gift of God's guidance because we are his sons. "For as many as are led of the Spirit of God, they are the Sons of God."[5] We *can know* God's will for our lives.

Another aspect of God's reputation is at stake here too, and that is his reputation as a prayer-answering God. As we have seen, Paul prayed for the Colossians to be filled with the knowledge of his will.[6] Epaphras joined him in prayer that they would "stand perfect and fully assured in all the

---

[4]Matthew 7:11 (NIV)
[5]Romans 8:14 (KJV)
[6]Colossians 1:9

He Will Be Our Guide

will of God."[7] Evidently they were both led of the Spirit to make those requests, since Paul was inspired of the Spirit to record them for our edification. Does God answer prayer? He claims to.[8] Will he answer this request for the knowledge of his will? He most certainly shall. His reputation as a God who answers prayer is in question.

You can pray confidently with the Psalmist, "Yes, you are my rock and my fortress; therefore for Your name's sake lead me and guide me."[9] And you can expect him to answer.

STANDING ON THE PROMISES

If the argument from God's nature is not conclusive enough, there is further evidence. We know that God will show us his plan for our lives simply because *he said he would*. Are you willing to take him at his word? The Bible is filled with promises of divine guidance. Let's look at a few.

"I will instruct you and teach you in the way which you should go;/I will counsel you with My eye upon you."[10] God uses three different words in that verse to reassure us that he will show us his will. He not only says that he will *teach* us or direct us in the way to go, but that he will *instruct* us in that way, meaning that he will cause us to understand it. Some people believe God is able to reveal his will, but they are not sure that they are capable of receiving it. God says he will make us capable; he will help us understand it.

Then he goes on to say he will *counsel* us with his eye upon us. He will give us perfect advice, then tenderly watch over us while we carry it out. What a fantastic promise! We would be foolish not to take him up on his offer.

And that is exactly what he says in the next verse. "Do not be as the horse or as the mule which have no understanding,/Whose trappings include bit and bridle to hold them in check,/Otherwise they will not come near to you."[11] I like being compared to a mule even less than being compared to

---

[7] Colossians 4:12 (NASB)
[8] Cf. Jeremiah 33:3; Matthew 7:7; John 14:13; et. al.
[9] Psalm 31:3 (Amp.)
[10] Psalm 32:8 (NASB)
[11] Psalm 32:9 (NASB)

a sheep. But that is what I am if I ignore God's guaranteed guidance.

How long is God willing to keep on showing us his will? The Psalmist says, "For this God is our God forever and ever; he will be our guide even unto death."[12] It matters not how old we are. He will keep on directing our paths to the very end of our lives.

"Well," you say, "that's a fine time to leave me—when I'm at death's door." But he doesn't leave us then. "You will keep on guiding me all my life with your wisdom and counsel; *and afterwards receive me into the glories of heaven!*"[13] When we exit from this earthly scene, he guides us right into his glorious presence for eternity. We couldn't ask for anything more marvelous than that.

The book of Proverbs contains some great promises of guidance. For example, in addition to the unequivocal assertion of Proverbs 3:6 that God will direct our paths, Solomon makes this interesting observation: "The way of the slothful man is a hedge of thorns: but the way of the righteous is made plain."[14] God illuminates the believer's path and shows him the way. That's the kind of God he is. We can count on him to make our pathway plain.

Isaiah can testify to that. "Thus says the Lord, your Redeemer, the Holy one of Israel: I am the Lord your God, who teaches you for your profit, who leads you in the way you should go."[15] You see, he is the God who leads.

Some still insist, "Well, he may lead others in the way they should go, but my life is too tangled and confused. There's no hope for me." Isaiah has a word for you too. "I will make the blind walk in a way that they do not know and lead them in paths unfamiliar to them. Darkness before them I will turn to light, and rough places I will make smooth."[16]

God is not willing to let you go on stumbling around in the dark. He wants to lead you into light. Satan knows that your life will bring glory to God when you know and do

---

[12] Psalm 48:14 (KJV)
[13] Psalm 73:24 (TLB)
[14] Proverbs 15:19 (KJV)
[15] Isaiah 48:17 (Berk.)
[16] Isaiah 42:16 (Berk.)

God's will, so he will try to keep you from it. But he cannot succeed if you do not let him. God's promises are firm: "I will lead," "I will guide," "I will make darkness into light." Believe him!

ACTIONS AND WORDS

"Promises, promises—they're nothing but words," you say. "I want to see action." Trace the history of God's dealings with men, and you will see illustration after illustration of God making known his will. Not only do his promises assure it and his character require it, but his actions prove it. Look at a few examples.

It wasn't easy for Abraham to leave his home town of Ur and take off for points unknown, but God promised to guide him to the place where he wanted him to settle.[17] And God did. When Abraham reached Canaan, God led him to a high hill and invited him to look out as far as he could see in every direction. Everything in sight was his. God had given it all to him and to his descendants.[18] He had been faithful to his promise. He had led him to the promised land.

Later Abraham sent his servant on a trip of 500 miles to find a bride for his son Isaac. And Abraham promised the servant that the angel of God would guide his way.[19] The man had no earthly idea for whom he was looking, but God led him to the precise girl he had prepared for Isaac. And he knew she was the one. The servant reported: "I bowed low and worshiped the Lord, and blessed the Lord, the God of my master Abraham, who had guided me in the right way to take the daughter of my master's kinsman for his son."[20] God was faithful to his promise.

Abraham's descendants later found themselves in Egyptian slavery, but God miraculously delivered them. Now they faced a dangerous trek through an unknown wilderness. How would they know the way? God promised to show

---
[17] Genesis 12:1
[18] Genesis 13:14, 15
[19] Genesis 24:7
[20] Genesis 24:48 (NASB)

them. And God did. He led them by a pillar of cloud during the day and a pillar of fire during the night.[21]

Centuries later, they found themselves in captivity again, this time in Babylon. But God moved the heart of a pagan king named Cyrus to release them and send them back to their land, and God led them home.

The Psalmist summed up God's faithfulness to the nation Israel through the years of their history like this: "And he led them forth by the right way, that they might go to a city of habitation. Oh that men would praise the Lord for his goodness, and for his wonderful works to the children of men!"[22]

Old Testament examples abound. But the New Testament has its outstanding illustrations as well. God supernaturally led a deacon named Philip from a successful evangelistic campaign in Samaria to a desert road near Gaza to witness to one lone Ethiopian.[23] Only God knows how great an impact that one man eventually made on his nation. We do know that Christianity was firmly planted in Ethiopia from the earliest years of church history. It may have been partially the result of that eunuch's faithful witness, and of Philip's openness to God's unmistakable leading.

Peter was led, contrary to all his natural impulses, to witness in the household of a Roman centurion.[24] And the gospel of Jesus Christ dramatically burst into the Gentile world for its first major penetration. The Spirit of God then led a group of prophets and teachers in Antioch to set Paul and Barnabas apart for special spiritual service.[25] And from that day forward the gospel of Jesus Christ began to penetrate the extremities of the known world. The roots of our own eternal salvation can be traced back to that particular revelation of God's will, for it launched the first full-scale foreign missionary program that eventually brought the gospel to us.

And now God wants to continue his work through us. We can know his plan for our lives. We are really no different from the Apostle Paul in this regard. God saved him to

[21]Exodus 13:21, 22
[22]Psalm 107:7, 8 (KJV)
[23]Acts 8:26
[24]Acts 10:19, 20
[25]Acts 13:1, 2

37 He Will Be Our Guide

"know his will,"[26] and he saved us for the same purpose. The writer to the Hebrews said that God can "equip you in every good thing to do His will, working in us that which is pleasing in His sight."[27]

[26] Acts 22:14 (KJV)
[27] Hebrews 13:21 (NASB)

CHAPTER 4
ONE STEP AT A TIME

We have learned from the Scriptures that God has a plan for our lives, that it includes every detail of daily living, and that we can know exactly what it is. Why is it, then, that so many Christians have so many questions about God's will? Why do they find it difficult to discern God's will and why do they lack the assurance that they are in his will?

As a pastor, I probably have more people come to me with questions about this subject than any other. I have come to the conclusion that some people may not yet have discovered God's plan because they are looking for the wrong thing. They may be expecting God to show them his blueprint for their whole life's building when he is trying to show them only the next board to hammer into place. They may be looking for a continent-wide road map when God simply wants to tell them which turn to take next.

If they have their minds set on seeing the whole picture, they are likely to overlook the next small detail of direction that God is trying to give them.

HEADLIGHTS ON THE HIGHWAY

The first basic principle of divine guidance is this: God leads us one step at a time. The Psalmist said, "The *steps* of a man are established by the Lord."[1] It is no accident that he used the word *steps* when he revealed the existence of God's plan for our lives. While God has the whole journey mapped out ahead of time, he conceives of that journey as a successive series of small steps, and that is the way he makes it known to us.

This foundational principle of guidance is graphically illustrated in another Psalm: "Your word is a lamp to my feet and a light to my path."[2] When an ancient traveler journeyed at night he carried an oil lamp with him. As he walked along, swinging the lamp out in front of him, he could see the rocks and ruts directly ahead of him in the road, and he could avoid them. Sometimes he actually strapped a small clay lamp to his ankle and it illuminated the path before him, one step at a time, as he walked. That is how God uses his Word to guide us. He does not promise a brilliant blaze of light to illuminate the road for miles ahead. He promises a lamp to our feet, enough light for the next step.

Maybe the illustration would be more meaningful in our mechanized society if we put it in terms of driving a car at night. The headlights on our automobiles do not expose the dangers a mile or so ahead. They merely divulge the next bend in the road. God knows that it may not be best for us to see too far down the highway of our lives. If he showed us the whole plan at the outset, we might decide that we do not want to follow it. It might involve more sacrifices than we are willing to make at this stage of our spiritual maturity, or it might look too difficult for us to handle at this point in our spiritual growth.

If God had told me when I was a student in college that I would someday pastor a large church and preach to thousands of people every Sunday, I probably would have laughed and said, "You'd better find somebody else for that plan, Lord. Make me a new one that is better suited to my personality and temperament." I would shake all over when I had to talk in front of a speech class of twenty students. Yet today there is nothing I would rather be doing than ministering the Word of God to hungry hearts.

[1] Psalm 37:23 (NASB)
[2] Psalm 119:105 (Amp.)

If God had told me that his plan to move me from a church in Texas to one in Alabama would eventually include an unpleasant church split and the beginning of a new local assembly, I probably would have said, "No thanks, Lord. I don't believe I'm up to that. I'll just stay where I am for a while and wait for another opportunity." But now as I look back on that experience from this vantage point, I would not trade it for anything. It did more to strengthen my faith in God's sovereign control of all things than any other episode in my life. Yet I can say with absolute certainty that I am glad I did not know where the road was leading when I took that step to Alabama.

Some steps are giant strides. One decision can commit us to a certain course for years to come, possibly for a lifetime. But however big it may be, it is still one single step. And it will be followed by many other single steps as we walk with the divine Shepherd day by day. If we run ahead of the light to see what lies beyond the next step, we shall find ourselves in the dark again.

The children of Israel were led through the wilderness on this day-by-day basis. They followed God's guiding cloud wherever it went. When it moved, they moved. When it stopped, they set up camp. If it remained one day, they stayed one day. If it remained a year, they stayed a year. But then when it lifted, they broke camp and followed.[3] They never knew for sure where it was taking them, but they trusted their faithful Shepherd to lead them in the right way. And their trust was never misplaced. He brought them safely to their promised land.

EXHIBIT A

This is the way God led the Apostle Paul as well. The day he met Christ, he asked, "What shall I do, Lord?" And the answer came back, "Arise and go on into Damascus; and there you will be told of all that has been appointed for you to do."[4] So he obeyed that command and took that one step to Damascus, and there God told him the general direction his

---

[3] Numbers 9:15–23
[4] Acts 22:10 (NASB)

life would take. He would be Christ's witness to all men of what he had seen and heard.[5]

But after that broad overview of God's plan for his future, the details came one step at a time. For example, three years after his conversion he went up to Jerusalem to meet the apostles and to witness to the Grecian Jews about Christ.[6] While he was there, he went into the Temple to pray and God spoke to him again: "Leave Jerusalem immediately, because they will not accept your testimony about me."[7]

Leaving made no sense at all to Paul. Everyone here knew how he had previously persecuted the Christians. Certainly they would believe that something supernatural had happened in his life and would accept his testimony. He tried to reason with God, but to no avail. The word came again: "Go, I will send you far away to the Gentiles."[8] So Paul took the next step in God's plan without any specific knowledge of where it would lead him, except that it would be to the Gentile world.

First God led him into Syria and Cilicia, where for several years he preached the gospel from his home town headquarters in Tarsus.[9] That's where Barnabas found him when he brought him to Antioch to assist in the ministry there.[10] That was to be the next place of service in the gradual revelation of God's plan.

ON THE ROAD

The next move was revealed when the Spirit of God spoke to the prophets and teachers at Antioch and instructed them to set Paul and Barnabas apart for special missionary service. There is no indication that they knew exactly where God wanted them to go, but he led them as they went. And when they returned to Antioch, "they gathered the church together and reported all that God had done through them and how

[5]Acts 22:15
[6]Acts 9:26–29; cf. also Galatians 1:18, 19
[7]Acts 22:18 (NIV)
[8]Acts 22:21 (NIV)
[9]Acts 9:30; Galatians 1:21–24
[10]Acts 11:25, 26

he had opened the door of faith to the Gentiles."[11] It was exciting to review how God had directed them step by step to the people who were ready to receive the message. Their experience was much like that of the old servant of Abraham looking for a bride for Isaac. He did not know exactly where he was going, but after he got there he could say confidently, "The Lord has guided me in the way."[12]

Another indication of God's step-by-step guidance in Paul's life occurred on his second missionary journey. Being commended to God's grace again by the leaders at Antioch, he traveled with Silas through Syria and Cilicia, strengthening the churches there. Then he revisited the churches which he had established in Galatia on his first journey.[13] After that we read, "Paul and his companions traveled throughout the region of Phrygia and Galatia, having been kept by the Holy Spirit from preaching the word in the province of Asia. When they came to the border of Mysia, they tried to enter Bithynia, but the Spirit of Jesus would not allow them to. So they passed by Mysia and went down to Troas."[14]

Do you see how they seemed to be feeling their way along, looking for opportunities, pushing on doors, backing off when the Spirit of God blocked their way? They wanted to do God's will and he was not going to let them make a mistake. He would not let them preach in Asia, and he would not even let them enter Bithynia. And at that point they did not know why. Maybe they thought that hearts there were not yet prepared for the message, or that some serious danger awaited them. But it is comforting to know that when we desire God's will above all else, he will see that we walk in it step by step, whether or not we know the reasons for our course.

NOTHING TO FEAR

Christians sometimes worry about the possibility of missing God's will. That cannot happen to anyone who truly wants

[11] Acts 14:27 (NIV)
[12] Genesis 24:27 (NASB)
[13] Acts 15:40—16:1
[14] Acts 16:6-8 (NIV)

to do his will. We can miss it by insisting on our own way, but not when we want only his way.

Isaiah assures us that even if we take a step in the wrong direction, he will call us back. "And if you leave God's paths and go astray, you will hear a Voice behind you say, 'No, this is the way; walk here.' "[15] The Psalmist agreed: "The Lord is good and glad to teach the proper path to all who go astray; he will teach the ways that are right and best to those who humbly turn to him."[16] Paul, too, certainly found this principle to be true. He greatly desired to preach the gospel in Bithynia, but he desired to do the will of God even more. So God kept him from making a costly mistake.

This disturbs and confuses some people in our day of goals and plans and management by objective. "How can we plan ahead if God leads us only one step at a time and sometimes blocks our way and sends us off in a different direction?"

Solomon gave us the answer to that one. "The mind of man plans his way,/But the Lord directs his steps."[17] We can make plans, seeking God's wisdom as we do so. But we must recognize that the plans we make are tentative at best. God may not give us clear direction about the specific details until we reach the crossroads and need to know which way to turn. Paul had a tentative strategy in mind when he left Antioch on that second missionary journey. But *his* plan was subject to the step-by-step revelation of *God's* plan.

Sometimes the disclosure of the next step may be more spectacular than it is on other occasions. That was the case with Paul's next move. "During the night Paul had a vision of a man of Macedonia standing and begging him, 'Come over to Macedonia and help us.' "[18] We shall discuss dreams and visions at greater length in a later chapter, but we mention this event here to show that God's direction into Europe was unmistakable. Paul needed to have that assurance, for he would be tempted to doubt God's leading after being severely beaten and clamped in stocks in a Philippian jail cell.

God never promised us that life in the center of his will

[15]Isaiah 30:21 (TLB)
[16]Psalm 25:8, 9 (TLB)
[17]Proverbs 16:9 (NASB)
[18]Acts 16:9 (NIV)

would be like a vacation on a South Pacific island. There will be problems. But along with the problems there will be peace, praise, and power. Paul and Silas sang God's praises in that prison and people came to know Christ.

RIGHT ON TIME

Whenever Paul needed direction, God was right there to provide it. He was never late. Opposition began to build against the gospel in Corinth on that second journey, and Paul was forced to leave the synagogue. He probably wondered whether he ought to stop preaching there and leave the city. He didn't have to wonder for long. "One night the Lord spoke to Paul in a vision: 'Do not be afraid; keep on speaking, do not be silent. For I am with you, and no one is going to attack and harm you, because I have many people in this city.' So Paul stayed for a year and a half, teaching them the word of God."[19] When the questions arose, the answers came—just when they were needed.

God did protect Paul from persecution during that extended ministry in Corinth. But it would not always be so. Near the end of his third missionary journey he had an opportunity to share some memorable truths with elders of the church at Ephesus. In the course of his message he said, "And now, compelled by the Spirit, I am going to Jerusalem, not knowing what will happen to me there. I only know that in every city the Holy Spirit warns me that prison and hardships are facing me."[20] Persecution was awaiting him, yet he had an unwavering confidence that the Holy Spirit was still directing him, step by step.

He was arrested in Jerusalem just as he had anticipated, and when he gave his defense before the Jewish Sanhedrin, they became so violent that the officer in charge thought they would tear him apart. But God was still guiding him. "The following night the Lord stood near Paul and said, 'Take courage! As you have testified about me in Jerusalem, so you must also testify in Rome.' "[21]

[19] Acts 18:9–11 (NIV)
[20] Acts 20:22, 23 (NIV)
[21] Acts 23:11 (NIV)

That promise sustained him through a dangerous conspiracy against his life, more than two years of imprisonment at Caesarea, repeated trials and interrogations before a succession of public officials, and a treacherous journey by sea that included a death-defying shipwreck. But he finally arrived in Rome and boldly testified about Jesus Christ, just as God promised he would.[22] The individual steps were sometimes surprising and sometimes painful, but the outcome was always satisfying because those steps were established by the Lord.

As I look back over my own life I see the same evidence of God's graduated guidance. As a high-schooler I told God I wanted to do his will, but I had no idea of what it might be. I felt a strong inclination to attend Wheaton College, and God made it possible against considerable human odds. After my first year, I chose to major in Bible, believing that God might lead me into some kind of Christian service career, but I had no knowledge at that time of what it might be.

During those years at Wheaton, God put Dallas Theological Seminary strongly on my mind, even though my teachers were recommending other seminaries and most of my friends were going elsewhere. But I felt an inner confidence and a settled peace about it. I knew it was the will of God. My aim at Dallas was to prepare myself more fully to serve the Lord, but I still did not know in what capacity that might be.

As graduation neared, some of my professors encouraged me to enter graduate school. I had no peace about further study without a regular ministry of some kind along with it, so my wife and I began to pray for God's decisive direction. Within weeks, a church in Fort Worth, which had been looking for an older and more experienced pastor for more than a year, finally decided to consider a recent seminary graduate and was given my name along with two others.

For no apparent reason, they began the candidating process with me, and after I had preached for them on two successive Sundays they voted to call me (by a fraction of a percentage point above what was required in their constitution and by-laws). So I found myself pastoring a church and working on a doctorate simultaneously. The doctoral work

---

[22]Acts 28:16, 30, 31

has long since been finished, but the pastoring has continued in the different locations of God's choosing, as he has directed one step at a time. Some instances of his guidance have been rather ordinary, others quite dramatic. I have seldom been able to see far ahead, but God has never failed to illuminate the next step because that is the way he leads.

Your experience may be similar. It certainly can be. Wherever you are at this moment in your Christian experience, God is ready to show you the next step in his plan for your life.

PART TWO
YOUR PERSONAL PREPARATION

CHAPTER 5
KNOWING THE SHEPHERD

Do you believe that God has a plan for your life, a plan which includes every detail of daily living? Do you believe that his plan is best for you, far superior to any plan you could design for yourself? Do you believe that God will show you that plan, step by step? If you want to know God's will in the decisions you face, then you must believe these things.

That was the first condition Solomon laid down in his magnificent promise of divine guidance: "Trust in the Lord with all your heart... and he will direct your paths."[1] Trust—faith—is essential. Without it there can be no guidance. And trust is our responsibility. In the first four chapters we have been discussing God's part, his plan for our lives, and his willingness to guide us. But there is some personal preparation which we must make before we shall be able to discern his guidance. That preparation will occupy our attention next.

Foremost in all the preparation is a believing heart. Most of us say that we want to do God's will and that we want to please him in every respect. We cannot do so without faith. "Without faith it is impossible to please him,"[2] said the writer to the Hebrews. We must believe that God is there,

---

[1] Proverbs 3:5, 6 (Berk.)
[2] Hebrews 11:6

that he is interested in leading us as individuals, and that we can safely entrust our lives to him. We must have implicit faith in our heavenly Father's wisdom, faithfulness, kindness, and love. Without such faith we would not even consider committing ourselves to his direction.

But trust demands knowledge. Some people seem to think faith is merely accepting what we cannot know. They think of faith as a shabby substitute for certain knowledge. "If you can't really know it," they say, "then take a blind leap in the dark and believe it anyway." That's not the way it is at all. True faith is built on accurate knowledge. If we do not know someone, we will find it very difficult to trust him.

Let me illustrate. My father was one of the first white men to visit the Auca Indians after Rachel Saint and Betty Elliot had settled in that tribe's territory and had begun working with them. While Dad was there, Kimo, one of the tribesmen who had participated in the murder of the five missionary men, offered to take him out into the jungle to show him how the Indians hunt monkeys with blow guns. Off they went, just the two of them.

Suddenly Dad realized that Kimo had disappeared. He called to him but there was no answer, only strange monkey sounds. Every time he called, the monkey sounds came from a different direction. Do you get the picture? My father was standing alone in the dense Ecuadorian jungle, while somewhere out of sight lurked a man who had been taught from his youngest days to kill foreigners. Would he revert to his old ways?

Dad admits to being a little afraid on that occasion—actually *terrified* might have been a better word than *afraid*. He and Kimo had not yet become bosom pals. Frankly, Dad didn't trust him. As it turned out, Kimo was playing games with him just to prove how helpless the white man was alone in the jungle. But it does exemplify the point. We cannot fully trust someone we do not fully know.

In this book we are talking about something far more serious than merely our physical well-being. The issue before us is our willingness to commit our entire future, for time and eternity, to One who offers to lead us only one step at a time, who does not show us his plan beforehand, nor tell us exactly where he is taking us. There is no way we can be expected to make such a commitment unless we get to know him intimately.

HOW WELL DO YOU KNOW HIM?

There is a sense in which every Christian knows the Lord. We often use the phrase *knows the Lord* synonymously with being born-again, with being a true Christian. Jesus said, "Now this is eternal life: that men may know you, the only true God, and Jesus Christ, whom you have sent."[3] Only by knowing God can we have eternal life. But there are degrees of knowledge. I am often asked to fill out a recommendation form for someone who is entering school or seeking a job. The form usually asks, "How well do you know the applicant?" Sometimes I must write, "casually"; and once in a while I must admit that I hardly know the person at all. I wonder where we would rate ourselves if we had to indicate on a questionnaire how well we know the Lord. Some of us would have to admit that it is only a very casual acquaintance. And some may hardly know him at all. That could be one reason we hesitate to trust him with our futures.

The children of Israel at Kadesh were a prime example of folks who did not trust God because they did not really know him. They refused to enter the land because of giants there, beside whom they said they looked like grasshoppers.[4] What a gross exaggeration! And God was on their side. What glaring ignorance of his greatness and power! But Joshua and Caleb knew God well. "The Lord loves us," they said. "He will bring us safely into the land and give it to us. . . . The Lord is with us and he has removed his protection from them! Don't be afraid of them."[5] But the people refused to listen, and failed to follow God's directive. The result was that they wandered aimlessly in the wilderness for forty years. Think of it. Forty years of misery simply because they had not taken the time to get to know their God.

Some of us, too, may be enduring the unhappiness which

[3]John 17:3 (NIV)
[4]Numbers 13:33
[5]Numbers 14:8, 9 (TLB)

Christians usually experience when they go their own way, and the reason could relate to this basic issue. We may never have taken the time to get to know God, and that's why we have not been willing to trust him with our lives.

It isn't God's fault that we fail to know him. He is making himself knowable to us in a myriad of ways. The only question is our response to his overtures. Put it in terms of a human relationship for a moment. Maybe you can remember someone trying to establish a friendship with you. He kept coming around, sharing more and more of his thoughts and feelings, hoping you would respond and share yourself with him. It made you ask yourself some questions and come to a decision. "Is this a person I really want to be close to? Do I care to expose my inner self to him? Am I willing to invest the time and effort which this friendship will demand?"

Most Christians face that same decision with God, particularly if they've gone to church routinely, read their Bibles a little, prayed some, but have engaged in no more meaningful communication with God than just that. The confrontation comes at different stages of growth in the lives of different believers, and it happens in different places and under different circumstances, but it is bound to occur.

One day we realize that God is trying to speak directly to us through his Word. He is telling us what he is like and what he wants to do for us. He may also be telling us what we are really like and what he expects from us. At that point we face a crucial decision: "Am I going to continue this mediocre level of Christian life, or am I going to cultivate and nurture my personal relationship with God and get to know him intimately?" We cannot take this decision lightly. Our whole future depends on it. Our willingness to entrust our lives to his guidance is inextricably bound up in how well we know him.

Sometimes God backs us against the wall in order to reveal himself to us. He did that to the children of Israel at the Red Sea. With no place to turn, and with the Egyptians bearing down on them from behind, they began to grumble and complain. "But Moses said to the people, 'Do not fear! Stand by and see the salvation of the Lord which He will accomplish for you today; for the Egyptians whom you have seen today, you will never see them again forever.' "[6] And God kept his promise. The Egyptians were defeated. God's people were delivered.

But even after their miraculous deliverance, they failed to believe God. Time after time they doubted him, and time after time he brought them to the end of their human resources so he could show himself strong on their behalf and prove to them his faithfulness. There is no better way for God to make known his power, his love, and his faithfulness, than in the trying situations of life.

One reason he allows us to experience problems like sickness, suffering, and sorrow, is so that he can reveal himself to us in the thick of the problem and we can come to know him in all of his fullness. He calls out to us lovingly and longingly in the middle of the crisis, "Be still, and know that I am God."[7] Only when we come to know him shall we be able to trust him with our lives. Every effort to discern the guidance of God must begin with knowing the guide.

BUT HE'S SO FAR AWAY

How can we get to know a God who lives in the heavens, who has no physical body that we can see or touch, and who does not speak to us in audible tones? There are two primary means—the Word and prayer. God tells us about himself in the Word. We can meditate on that truth and respond to him in prayer and praise. The purpose of this interpersonal communion, as J. I. Packer puts it, is "to clear one's mental and spiritual vision of God, and to let His truth make its full and proper impact on one's mind and heart."[8] Through it we come to know him.

If we want to get to know God, then we must begin by reading our Bibles with our spiritual ears tuned to everything God says about himself. A good place to begin is in the Psalms. "The Lord is my rock, and my fortress, and my deliverer."[9] "The Lord is my light and my salvation."[10] "God is

[6]Exodus 14:13 (NASB)
[7]Psalm 46:10 (KJV)
[8]J. I. Packer, *Knowing God*, (InterVarsity Press, 1973), p. 19
[9]Psalm 18:2 (KJV)
[10]Psalm 27:1 (KJV)

our refuge and strength, a very present help in trouble."[11] Knowing things like these about him will help us trust him. And trusting him will prove him true, causing our faith to grow even more.

Meditate on the attributes of God as they are revealed in the Word. God is *everywhere*.[12] Wherever he leads us, he will go along with us. God is *all-knowing*.[13] He even declares the end from the beginning.[14] It isn't hard to trust someone who knows how everything is going to turn out. God is *all-powerful*.[15] He is able to solve every problem we face as we live in the center of his will. God is *love*.[16] We can be assured that whatever he asks us to do or wherever he directs us to go, the experiences we find there will be an expression of his love for us. God is *good*.[17] The way that he leads has to be best for us. God is *faithful*.[18] He will never fail us as we follow his guidance. There is no end to God's revelation of himself in the Word. It is an inexhaustible mine of truth. Dig out more and more, and get to know him better and better.

Something will happen to us as we get to know God better. The more clearly we see him in all his glory, the more clearly we shall see ourselves in our true condition—weak, lowly, sinful, blind, and helpless; and consequently, the more intensely we shall sense our need for him. When we recognize how inadequate we are in and of ourselves, and how sufficient and strong he is, we shall be more willing to trust him with our lives.

There is yet another reason for getting into the Scriptures as we seek to know the Lord and to do his will. Listening to him speak to us through the Word will familiarize us with the sound of his voice.

Many voices will clamor to be heard in the perplexity of a difficult decision. How shall we recognize the voice of God? There is only one way—by the familiarity which comes

[11] Psalm 46:1 (KJV)
[12] Psalm 139:7-12
[13] Psalm 147:5
[14] Isaiah 46:10
[15] Jeremiah 32:17
[16] 1 John 4:16
[17] Psalm 119:68
[18] Lamentations 3:23

through repeated exposure and experience. A child knows his parent's voice because he hears it every day. I particularly remember a distinctive whistle my father developed. It was not loud or shrill, yet I could find him in a crowd of a thousand people if I could hear that familiar whistle.

A sheep knows his shepherd's voice because he hears it every day. Jesus said, "My sheep hear my voice, and I know them, and they follow me."[19] How do we gain that kind of familiarity with our shepherd? Jesus gave us the answer while he was talking to a group of unbelieving Jews one day. "You diligently study the Scriptures because you think that by them you possess eternal life. These are the Scriptures that testify about me . . ."[20] God reveals himself through the Scriptures, his own inspired Word. That Word originates in the breath of his mouth.[21] We will learn to recognize his voice as we spend time in his Word.

TALKING BACK

But there is at least one additional important step to knowing God. After hearing what he has said to us in the Word, we must prayerfully meditate on it, mull it over in our minds, think through its ramifications, then apply it to the various details of personal living. As we see its implications, we praise God for the truth he has shown us, we share with him our innermost thoughts and feelings about it, and we seek his strength to put it into practice. The real measure of our knowledge of God is not how many facts we know about him or how much activity we carry on for him. It is, as Packer aptly puts it, "how we pray and what goes on in our hearts."[22]

Some Christians spend very little time in God's presence, but they certainly run to him for guidance when a crisis strikes. "Uh, haven't been here much lately, Lord, but I gotta make this decision by noon today. Think you could tell me what to do just this once? I promise I'll get started with my

---

[19] John 10:27 (KJV)
[20] John 5:39, 40 (NIV)
[21] Matthew 4:4; 2 Timothy 3:16
[22] Packer, op. cit., p. 27

quiet time again next week." But guidance doesn't come that way. There is something more important to God than that we know his will; it is that we know *him*. And the only way we shall be prepared to discern his will when decisions confront us is to begin spending time in his presence *now*.

When two people love one another and live in each other's company, they grow to understand each other's wishes. As their relationship grows more intimate, their knowledge of one another's desires becomes more complete. My wife and I are far more sensitive to each other's needs today than we were the day we got married. Our intimate fellowship over the years has resulted in an expanding knowledge. I'm beginning to know her wants and wishes before she ever expresses them, and she is beginning to know mine.

Would you like to know what God wants you to do? Then begin by getting to *know him*. Spend time in his Word. Share your soul with him in prayer. As the prophet Hosea put it, "Oh, that we might know the Lord! Let us press on to know him, and he will respond to us as surely as the coming of dawn or the rain of early spring."[23]

---

[23] Hosea 6:3 (TLB)

CHAPTER 6
NOT MY WILL

Horses and mules have never been famous for their cooperative spirit. They may know you well enough to have no reason to doubt you when you give them directions. Yet they have a problem: their own indomitable, stubborn self-will. It is always there and you never know when or how it will erupt. The horse may express it by refusing to stop. Sometimes he starts galloping home toward the barn and there is nothing you can do to stop him or to change his direction. The mule usually expresses it by refusing to go. You can pull him, push him, whip him, or tease him with carrots, but at times he simply will not budge. Neither one of them can ever know the destination to which you want them to go, nor what you will allow them to do there, while they are exerting their own will.

That is exactly why God said, "Do not be as the horse or as the mule which have no understanding."[1] The greatest obstacle to knowing God's plan for our lives is the persistence of our own unbending purposes and preferences.

Dealing with that stubborn will may be the most important single factor in discerning and doing the will of God. How can we deal with it? The answer was most lucidly given by the Apostle Paul: "Therefore, I urge you, brothers,

---

[1] Psalm 32:9 (NASB)

in view of God's mercy, to offer yourselves as living sacrifices, holy and pleasing to God—which is your spiritual worship. Do not conform any longer to the pattern of this world, but be transformed by the renewing of your mind. Then you will be able to test and approve what God's will is—his good, pleasing and perfect will."[2]

LIVING SACRIFICES

The subject of these verses is finding the will of God. More specifically, the subject is testing and approving what God's will is—discerning his will accurately in our experience and accepting it as the only tried and proven way to live. Paul established two basic criteria for such an experiential involvement in the will of God. The first one is *presentation* and the second is *transformation*. Let us look at the first one in this chapter.

"I urge you," says Paul, ". . . to offer yourselves as living sacrifices." That word *offer* literally means "to place beside." It was used of a worshiper placing his sacrificial animal on the altar as an act of consecration to God. To offer that animal in sacrifice was to give it up completely to God, to surrender all rights to use it as the offerer pleased. It was no longer his but God's. God had the prerogative of doing anything he pleased with it.

In the same spirit, God wants us to offer him our bodies, not to be killed and burned on an altar, but as "living sacrifices." He wants all the rights to our total person. He wants the privilege of doing with us as he pleases. "Give me your body," he says, "so I can use it as the vehicle for accomplishing my will." And with our bodies goes everything we are and have—our time, our abilities, our resources, our personalities, our plans, our desires, our aspirations, our affections. He wants us to give them all to him to use as he desires.

He isn't going to force us to do that. He will not invade our lives and brutally take control of us. He asks us to offer ourselves voluntarily in grateful response to the boundless

[2]Romans 12:1, 2 (NIV)

mercy he has extended to us in Christ. If we want to know his will, then we must become his living sacrifices.

UNCLE SAM WANTS YOU!

But the word *offer* also meant "to place at one's disposal, to be there to help." It was used of a servant who was completely at his master's disposal, whose will was always subordinate to his master's wishes. There was no point in a master's telling his servant what he wanted him to do unless he was assured that the servant would do it. A profitable servant had to be totally available to do his master's bidding. Paul is urging us to make ourselves that available to God. And unless God can be assured that we will carry out his directions, there is really no good reason for him to tell us what those directions are.

Suppose for a moment that you are standing in a recruiting office of the United States Army. While the modern army gives you some choice before you join, there is a great deal the recruiter is not going to tell you. There will be hundreds of directives issued throughout the course of your military career, but he isn't going to stand there and try to explain to you every detail of the army's plan for your life, every place they're going to send you, and everything they're going to ask you to do. That would be absurd. When Uncle Sam says, "I want you," he means that he wants an unconditional surrender of your entire being to him. And not until you make that commitment and put yourself at the army's disposal will the entire plan begin to unfold for you.

God wants you far more than Uncle Sam does. God urges you, begs you, beseeches you, pleads with you to offer yourself to him. And the tense of the verb *offer* indicates that the presentation he seeks is a decisive and determinative act that takes place at one crucial point in time, similar to signing the dotted line in the recruiter's office. It's like saying, "Here's my life, Lord. There are lots of things I would like to do with it, but what you want me to do is more important than all of my wishes. I am putting myself completely at your disposal for the rest of my life."

SOMETHING TO DO

Not many of us think that far ahead when we come to God for guidance. We pray rather glibly, "Lord, show me your will," but we forget that God requires us first to put ourselves at his permanent command. This lifelong commitment may be the only way he can be sure we will do his will after he has revealed it to us.

You see, God's will is something to *do*, not just something to know. There are more references in Scripture to doing God's will than to knowing it. In fact, the Apostle James warned us that knowing it without doing it is sin.[3] And when we want to do it as much as we want to know it, God assures us that we shall know it. Surrender is the key to knowing God's will.

Jesus affirmed this principle as well. The Jews were wondering how he knew so much theology, having never attended their rabbinical schools. So he told them. His doctrine was not his; it originated with the one who sent him. And then he told them how they could be sure it came from God. "If any man is willing to do His will, he shall know of the teaching, whether it is of God, or whether I speak from Myself."[4]

While that statement in John 5 refers primarily to his Word, it also applies to his will, since his will is revealed through his Word. How can we know whether we are being led by God or by our own desires? How can we know that our directions are from God? The answer Jesus gave is simply this: if our desire is to do his will rather than our own, *we shall know*.

Countless Christians through the centuries have testified to the validity of Jesus' principle. When they have become absolutely certain that they wanted to do God's will, regardless of their own personal preferences and regardless of what his will might be, then guidance has come. And continual guidance comes to those who have completely yielded themselves to and are continually controlled by his indwelling Spirit.

---

[3]James 4:17
[4]John 5:17 (NASB)

Others may find direction sporadically and in isolated instances, but only those who have settled this matter for life can be sure of walking uninterruptedly in the center of God's plan. The surrender of our wills to Jesus Christ is the most important decision we will ever face after we have trusted him as Savior from sin.

The Psalmist established the same basic prerequisite for divine guidance in Old Testament times. "The meek will he guide in judgment; and the meek will he teach his way."[5] Meekness involves surrendering the right to run our own lives. It involves the removal of selfishness and pride. It involves a broken and a contrite heart, a teachable spirit. The teachable person is obviously the one to whom God can teach his ways.

When most of us face a decision, that decision itself is usually uppermost in our minds—where we're supposed to go and what we're supposed to do. But God is more interested in the condition of our hearts. He is interested in the absence of our stubborn self-will, and in our genuine willingness to do his bidding. The idea is repeated several verses later: "Who is the man who fears the Lord? He will instruct him in the way he should choose."[6] To fear God is to reverence him, to be humble and teachable before him. The price of knowing God's will is the total surrender of our lives to him.

DISCOUNT PRICES

Some of us have developed clever ways to avoid paying the full price. One method is to decide what we want to do, then tell God we're going to do it for him. We take out a mental piece of paper, draw up the blueprint we want, and then ask God to get out his rubber stamp and mark it *Approved*. "God, I'm going to be a successful businessman. I'm going to make lots of money and give it to missions. I'm going to be active in my church. I'm going to witness to my business associates. I'm going to speak at evangelistic banquets. I want you to bless me."

[5]Psalm 25:9 (KJV)
[6]Psalm 25:12 (NASB)

Or maybe it will sound more pious than that: "Lord, I'm going to be a missionary. I plan to go to a part of the world that has never had a witness and I'm going to pioneer the gospel there and build a great work for you. And I want you to bless me." That's not what God wants at all. He want us to hand him a blank piece of paper, figuratively speaking, and say, "Here, Lord. You fill it in for me. I will do anything you ask."

Another favorite ploy is to attach a few strings to our commitment. We say to God, "I'll do anything, but . . ." We mean, "I'll go anywhere you want me to go but to Lower Slobovia." "I'll do anything you want me to do but give up Zeb." "I'll work with anybody you want me to work with except lepers." "I'll be anything you want me to be except the church custodian."

But God is the potter and we are the clay. He wants us to be totally pliable in his hands. And unless we remove the restrictions, we may never find out what he does want us to do.

Sometimes we bargain with God. "OK, Lord, I'll be a missionary if you let me marry Eloise." Or, "I'll take that job, Lord, if it will pay some overtime." That's the kind of stunt Jacob tried to pull with God. Jacob said, "If God will help and protect me on this journey and give me food and clothes, and will bring me back safely to my father, then I will choose Jehovah as my God! And this memorial pillar shall become a place for worship; and I will give you back a tenth of everything you give me!"[7]

God isn't very excited about that kind of relationship. He wants to be Lord of our lives. It took a wrestling match with Jacob and a dislocated thigh before God got him to surrender his stubborn will.[8]

Sometimes we ask God to show us his will, and we think we want to do it, but deep in our hearts we know that we may not do it at all if we don't like what he indicates. We already know what we want to do and we're actually looking for God to validate our will. Jeremiah ministered to people like that, and what a heartbreaking experience it was! They

[7] Genesis 28:20-22 (TLB)
[8] Cf. Genesis 32:24-32

wanted to flee to Egypt to escape the wrath of Nebuchadnezzar, king of Babylon, but they decided they should find out what God wanted them to do first. So they said to Jeremiah, "Beg the Lord your God to show us what to do and where to go."[9] They even added, "Whether we like it or not, we will obey the Lord our God."[10]

It all sounded so sincere that Jeremiah inquired of the Lord, who told him the people should stay in Judah. Jeremiah relayed that information to them but suddenly they were singing another tune. "You lie! The Lord our God hasn't told you to tell us not to go to Egypt!"[11] ". . . and all the people refused to obey the Lord and stay in Judah."[12]

An Old Testament soothsayer named Balaam was another notorious example of a man who asked God what he should do when he knew all along what his own plan would be. Messengers from the king of Moab wanted him to go with them and curse Israel. God said, "Don't go with them."[13] That was clear and decisive direction from the Lord. Yet when the messengers of the king came back to plead some more and to offer him more money, Balaam answered, "Stay here tonight so that I can find out whether the Lord will add anything to what he said before."[14] He wanted that money which the king had offered, and he was trying to badger God into approving his own personal plan to get it.

We do it too! We ask God to show us his will when we already know what we're going to do. We just want to check God's plan to see if we like it any better than our own. And if we don't, we go our own way. We think we will be happier on the path of our own choosing.

But it can never be so. "Before every man there lies a wide and pleasant road he thinks is right, but it ends in death."[15] We cannot live to please ourselves and still expect the blessing of God upon us. Except in rare instances, such as with Balaam and with people of Jeremiah's day, God seldom

[9]Jeremiah 42:3 (TLB)
[10]Jeremiah 42:6 (TLB)
[11]Jeremiah 43:2 (TLB)
[12]Jeremiah 43:4 (TLB)
[13]Numbers 22:12
[14]Numbers 22:19 (TLB)
[15]Proverbs 16:25 (TLB)

gives directions when he knows we will not follow them.

The supreme example of doing the Father's will was the Lord Jesus Christ. "I do not seek My own will," he said, "but the will of Him who sent Me."[16] And it was no empty claim. He proved it when he faced the most awesome and fearful experience of all human history, that of bearing the punishment for the whole world's sin. With utter self-renunciation he declared, "Not my will, but yours be done."[17] He blazed the trail before us. Now through the strength which he supplies, we may follow in his steps.[18]

WHAT ABOUT MY DESIRES?

Does this mean that we must annihilate all of our own wishes and desires, destroy every thought of what we might like to do? I don't think it is even possible to do that. Jesus himself admitted that his desires were different from his Father's when he said, "Father, if you are willing, take this cup from me."[19] And I cannot find any reference to God requiring us to remove every trace of personal desire from our hearts. He simply asks that we be willing to subordinate our desires to his, just as Jesus did.

There is no danger in such subordination. God does not take pleasure in denying us what we want. His will for us may be the very thing we love to do best, and he may reveal his plan to us through those personal desires. He just wants us to be willing to go anywhere, to do anything, to make any sacrifice he asks. He may ask us to give him something, then turn right around and give it back to us, as he did with Abraham when the old patriarch proved his readiness to offer his son Isaac. But he wants us to demonstrate that we are willing.

Some people hold back from yielding their lives to the Lord because they are afraid he might demand more of them than they are willing to give. They are sure he will ask them to give up everything they enjoy, and do everything they

[16]John 5:30 (NASB)
[17]Luke 22:42 (NIV)
[18]Cf. 1 Peter 2:21
[19]Luke 22:42 (NIV)

despise, as if he were some sort of celestial crank who delights in making everybody miserable. They envision themselves ending up single and lonely, wading through alligator-infested jungle swamps or getting cooked in some hungry cannibal's caldron. But God isn't out to get us. He enjoys giving us good things.[20] He takes pleasure in giving us the desires of our hearts.[21] To the Jewish captives in Babylon he sent this heartening message which we can appropriate to ourselves: "For I know the plans I have for you, says the Lord. They are plans for good and not for evil, to give you a future and a hope."[22] The Psalmist said, "And when we obey him, every path he guides us on is fragrant with his lovingkindness and his truth."[23]

If we are truly yielded to him, he will take away the desires that are contrary to his and give us new desires that are consistent with his. As the Apostle Paul declared, "It is God who is at work in you, both to will and to work for His good pleasure."[24] We cannot lose by yielding. God either gives us what we desire or in due time plants new desires in our hearts. But when our wills are genuinely surrendered to Christ, we can actually do what we want to do with the assurance that we are in the will of God.

Following God's plan is never a drag; it is always our highest joy and pleasure. God's will is "acceptable."[25] The word means "pleasing"—pleasing both to God and to us. As Jesus pointed out to his disciples beside a well in Sychar, doing God's will can be more satisfying than a delicious dinner.[26] Resisting God's will is a sure road to misery, but surrender brings happiness and delight.

When you present yourself to God for him to use as he chooses, you may find that your new attitude of submissiveness brings an immediate end to your struggle to know his will. That's what happened with Isaiah. God spoke to him saying, "Whom shall I send, and who will go for us?" Isaiah,

[20]Cf. Romans 8:32; James 1:17
[21]Psalm 37:4
[22]Jeremiah 29:11 (TLB)
[23]Psalm 25:10 (TLB)
[24]Philippians 2:13 (NASB)
[25]Romans 12:2 (KJV)
[26]John 4:34

responding before he knew any of the details of God's plan, laid his life on the line. "Here am I," he said, "send me."[27] And immediately the will of God began to unfold before him.[28]

Are you ready to put yourself at God's disposal, yield your will to him, offer yourself as a living sacrifice? Tell him right now that you are willing to do anything he desires, whatever it costs you. This may be an emotional experience for some. For others it may be a calm and quiet transaction. But it is essential if we are ever to follow God's plan for our lives. You may want to write the date of your surrender in your Bible so you will never forget it. You will certainly want to live every day in the light of your commitment, telling God anew each morning of your willingness to do whatever he desires for you that day. Then each sunrise will begin a fresh adventure of walking in the will of God.

[27]Isaiah 6:8 (KJV)
[28]Cf. verse 9 ff.

CHAPTER 7
THE RENEWED MIND

"How can I be absolutely certain that I *want* to do God's will?" Sharon was a college student who had come to my office for counsel concerning her future. She was earnestly seeking the will of God, but she doubted her own yieldedness to Christ. "Am I really willing to do anything he asks? I think I am, but how can I be sure?"

Her question has been asked by many Christians at some point in their lives. If knowing the will of God depends on our total surrender to him, how can we be sure we have actually done it and meant it? The answer comes to light where Paul explains another essential prerequisite for discovering God's plan for our lives, that of *transformation*. "Do not conform any longer to the pattern of this world, but be transformed by the renewing of your mind. Then you will be able to test and approve what God's will is—his good, pleasing and perfect will."[1]

DOING YOUR OWN THING

The first thing Paul mentions in this verse is our tendency to conform to the philosophy of this age. This tendency constitutes a pressure against transformation. The word *conform*

[1] Romans 12:2 (NIV)

means to fashion or shape one thing like another, particularly in its outward appearance. Phillips' now famous paraphrase still conveys the idea best: "Don't let the world around you squeeze you into its own mold." The tense Paul used indicates that this is the very thing we are prone to do. He said literally, "Stop being fashioned by this age."

If we have yielded our wills to Christ, Satan is going to try to water down our decision by subtly introducing traces of self-will. Before we met Christ we operated exclusively on that basis. That's the only way the people of the world know how to live. They do not even think about doing the will of God. They do as they please, "fulfilling the desires of the flesh and of the mind."[2] Satan wants us to revert to that basic life style, that "do your own thing" philosophy of this age. And in his attempt to push us into the world's mold he attacks us from within and attacks us from without.

For one thing, Satan uses our emotional immaturity and our personality defects to cloud our commitment to Christ and to confuse our understanding of his will. A Christian psychiatrist, writing on the will of God, has explained how childhood conflicts which were never resolved can lodge in our subconscious and affect our decisions.[3] Something such as the unfulfilled need for parental affection could cause us to jump into an unwise marriage. Or resentment against a parent could result in our shutting out of our lives someone else with similar traits, without our ever consciously recognizing why we did it.

Defense mechanisms help us rationalize our erroneous and childish ways of thinking, so that we fool ourselves into believing that what we are doing is actually God's way. We may need professional counsel to uncover these subconscious conflicts. But in many cases an honest admission of what God has said in his Word would expose our self-deception, and an honest surrender to Christ would make us put away our rationalizations and help us conform to God's way instead of our own.

But the temptation to succumb to our own desires is going

---

[2]Ephesians 2:3 (KJV)
[3]Marion H. Nelson, *How to Know God's Will* (Moody Press, 1963), pp. 24–35.

to be a daily battle. Satan will see to that. In addition to these areas of immaturity, his arsenal will include an infinite variety of fleshly motives by which he will try to lure us away from God's will. *Money* is one of his favorites. We say it doesn't affect our decisions, but it does. "A man has to provide for his family," we protest. Sure he does! The Scripture establishes that principle.[4] But the primary issue in a decision is simply what God wants us to do, not how much money it pays. If we are doing what he desires, he will see that our needs are met.

Other considerations that may also muddle the issue include the prestige of position, or the possibility for advancement, or the potential for praise and commendation, or mere convenience or personal advantage. The desire to escape some unpleasant situation may influence us too. Even the weather could become a determining factor. Climate is important to unbelievers when they consider a relocation, and Christians may let it color their thinking as well.

"But we're in love," is probably the greatest rationalization of all when it comes to discerning God's will in marriage. That ecstatic state of hormonal magnetism which is often mistaken for true love has been used to justify a great many mismatched marriages that have dishonored the Lord. But that is the basis on which the *world* operates, and we must not be pushed into its mold. God knows whether we have true love, which lives for the happiness of its object, or merely infatuation, which seeks happiness for itself. And he can help us determine which it is if we are willing to know. "All the ways of a man are clean in his own sight, but the Lord weighs the motives."[5]

Maybe we should cultivate the habit of asking ourselves why we think a particular course of action is right, and then list the reasons. We may be surprised to see how many reasons on our list are the same ones the people of the world would give. God says, "Stop being fashioned by this world."

It's easy to see rationalizations in the lives of other Christians, yet it's difficult to recognize them in our own. But God's help is available. With the Psalmist we can pray,

[4] 1 Timothy 5:8
[5] Proverbs 16:2 (NASB)

"Search me, O God, and know my heart; test my thoughts. Point out anything you find in me that makes you sad, and lead me along the path of everlasting life."[6]

In addition to these attacks from within, Satan relentlessly bombards us from without—with his attempts to implant the philosophy of the world in our minds. He uses every possible means at his disposal—television, radio, newspapers, magazines, books, motion pictures, music, unbelieving friends, loved ones, fellow workers. Sometimes he even uses Christians, particularly carnal Christians. We hear so much that contradicts God's Word from so many different sources that we soon begin to accept the world's standard and doubt God's.

For example, the world says that you can always divorce your mate if your marriage does not work out well. The message is repeated until we begin to believe it. Christian parents may even say it: "Divorce him; he's nothing but a bum." And so, without any biblical grounds, a Christian may take the easy way out. It seems so much simpler than working at the marriage, giving up personal rights, swallowing pride, and giving one's self sacrificially for the good of the mate and the marriage.

And again, the world keeps talking about the alleged merits of living together without marriage. They keep saying it and saying it until Christian young people begin to think that God can't really mean what he says in his Word. They begin to think that God's Word is outdated and irrelevant. So they enter into a sinful relationship which God warns will leave scars on their souls and disrupt their lives for years to come. If we ever hope to find God's plan for our lives, we must stop being fashioned by the people of the world and by the philosophy of the age.

COME OUT OF YOUR COCOON

Paul turns now from the negative prohibition to a positive plea for transformation: "But be transformed," he exhorts. The word he uses means "to change into another form." We

[6]Psalm 139:23, 24 (TLB)

get our English word *metamorphosis* from it. God wants us to undergo a complete metamorphosis of inward character which finds expression in a different kind of outward conduct, much as a caterpillar is transformed into a beautiful floating butterfly. And the tense here indicates a continuous process. Day after day we are to be experiencing continual changes that bring us progressively into the likeness of Christ.[7]

The lives of Christians are to be different! They are to be marked by increasing obedience to the Word of God. And we shall not be able to discern God's guidance apart from this kind of transformed living. Why should God reveal his will to us in matters not specifically mentioned in his Word when we have shown little interest in obeying what he has already revealed? It's not fair of us to ask him for direction in one matter when we have willfully rejected his clear direction in other matters.

We pray, "Lord, show me your will." But he has already shown it to us in areas which we may have conveniently ignored. And we cannot discover the next step in his plan for our lives until we demonstrate our sincerity by obeying what we already know. The key to knowing the will of God is not only a decisive act of surrender, but also a daily life of obedience.

We have a tendency to seek God's will for big decisions of life such as schooling, marriage, vocation or an important relocation, but neglect him in the many little issues he talks about in his Word. This may indicate that our motive is not to please him, but merely to avoid the unpleasantness that inevitably accompanies a major mistake.

One man asked his Christian friends to pray with him about accepting a new job offer. He said he wanted to do God's will. It was later revealed that he had been slipping items into his pockets at the end of each workday and bringing them home with him. He didn't want to do God's will at all, at least not to please the Lord. He just didn't want to get stuck with a new job that was worse than the one he had. His motives were selfish.

---

[7]Cf. 2 Corinthians 3:18 where this same word is used.

That man knew very little about transformed living. God says, "He who has been stealing must steal no longer."[8] If that man really wanted to do God's will he would have stopped taking things that didn't belong to him, acknowledged his sin and made restitution for everything he had taken. To request divine guidance about a job offer before he had done that was outright hypocrisy.

Christians are told to "walk in the light,"[9] which means walking in obedience to God's Word. Paul says, "Walk as children of light... Proving what is acceptable unto the Lord."[10] Interestingly enough, the words *proving* and *acceptable* here are the very same Greek words used in Romans 12:2 about God's will. The apostle is affirming that we must be walking in the light of God's Word if we wish to discern the will of God.

Did you ever get lost in a strange place and then try to follow somebody's directions in the dark? It's almost impossible. Just so, the darkness of sin clouds our ability to distinguish God's guidance. We must be living in obedience to the Word of God.

Some folks may be getting discouraged by now. "How can I ever know God's plan for my life if first I must be obeying everything the Word says? I don't even know everything it says, or all that God expects from me." Don't be discouraged. Nobody else does either. We're all still learning, and God doesn't expect any finite human being to know everything. As we learn one truth from the Word, we claim his grace to obey it and we make it a part of our daily lives. Then we learn another truth and build that one into our habit pattern of daily living. That is spiritual growth, and by that process our lives are gradually transformed.

Are you beginning to see the answer to Sharon's opening question? How can we be sure we really want to do God's will? *By doing what we already know to be his will!* The more important question is not, "What does God want me to do with my future?" It is, "Am I living as God wants me to

[8]Ephesians 4:28 (NIV)
[9]1 John 1:7
[10]Ephesians 5:8, 10 (KJV)

live today?" When we get today squared away, we can rest assured that God will guide us tomorrow.

REPROGRAM THE COMPUTER

If transformed living is a vital key to knowing God's will, then we need to know how we can be changed. Paul next shares God's plan for our transformation. It is by *the renewing of our minds.*

Medical science has long suggested that the human mind is like a giant computer. The readout which determines our behavior will be the direct result of what we feed into it. If we want to live differently, we will need to reprogram the computer, make the mind new by feeding into it new information by which we can process the decisions of life. That new information is obviously the growth-inducing Word of God. The counsel of the Apostle Peter, for example, is: "Like newborn babes, long for the pure milk of the word, that by it you may grow in respect to salvation."[11]

This will necessitate a systematic program of Bible memorization. We will not get the proper readout unless the information is permanently stored in the computer's memory bank. Hearing the Word is not enough. Most of us are rather forgetful. We must learn the Word, inscribe it indelibly on our souls.

But memorizing Scripture is not enough in itself either. We can know Bible facts and recite Bible verses without having a renewed mind and a transformed life. We must learn to appropriate those facts to our lives, examine their relevance to the various aspects of daily living, and then apply them when the suitable occasion arises.

Some Christians have read their Bibles and listened to sermons for years with their minds out of gear. They have never honestly applied the truth to their manner of living. They are basically moral and ethical people. They comply with the will of God in certain practices because that is the way they were taught and that is the way they have always

---

[11] 1 Peter 2:2 (NASB)

lived. But they are not growing. In other ways they still conform to the world because they have not let God reprogram their minds with his Word.

Every day we face numerous choices in which the action we take will be determined by the way our minds are programmed. Let us assume, for instance, that a young man ambles into a drugstore to pick up a tube of toothpaste. His eye catches the newsstand with its alluring array of nude girlie magazines. Will he take a few minutes to feed the flesh or will he resist that temptation by the power of God's indwelling Spirit? If his mind is programmed with the philosophy of this age, he will probably go right ahead and enjoy an uninterrupted lust break. After all, who is he hurting? Nobody in sight even knows him. But if he is programmed with God's perspective, he will resist, for Jesus said that anyone who looks at a woman lustfully has already committed adultery with her in his heart.[12]

Or suppose the girls at school are sitting around the lounge engaged in a good old-fashioned gabfest. The name of one of their "friends" comes up for discussion and some rather unflattering information is aired. You happen to know something about her that would contribute beautifully to the trend of the conversation. Will you share it or will you claim God's grace to change the subject to something more beneficial? If you are programmed with the philosophy of the world, you won't hesitate to tell all. But if God's Word has been molding your mind, you will endeavor to direct the conversation toward more profitable matters. "Do not let any unwholesome talk come out of your mouths, but only what is helpful for building others up according to their needs, that it may benefit those who listen."[13]

Maybe you as a hard-working man come home from the office frazzled from a difficult day of dealing with people. There is nothing you want more than to relax with that ball game on TV. Much to your dismay, you find your wife discouraged and depressed. "Honey," she says, "I need your help tonight. Will you please spend some time talking to me? I just need to talk." If you are programmed with the

[12] Matthew 5:28 (NIV)
[13] Ephesians 4:29 (NIV)

philosophy of this age you will probably say, "Are you kidding? Not tonight! These are the play-offs. You can straighten yourself out if you want to." But if you are programmed with the Word of God and have thought through the implications of loving your wife as Christ loved the church,[14] your reaction will be different. You will probably say something like, "I want to do everything I can to help you. Let's sit down and talk. You're far more important to me than a ball game."

Or suppose you are strolling through a department store and you spot a beautiful lamp. "Oh, that's just what I've been looking for. It will go perfectly in my living room." But it costs so much you know that if you buy that lamp you will need to cut your giving to the Lord's work this month, and you may not be able to pay the man who repaired your refrigerator. If you are programmed with the philosophy of this age you will probably buy the lamp and tell yourself that somebody else will support the Lord's work, and that the repairman can certainly wait one more month to get paid. You may even put it on your credit card and increase the agony by adding interest charges. But if you are programmed with "Owe no man anything,"[15] and "Each man should give what he has decided in his heart to give,"[16] you will probably do without the lamp. You don't really need it.

God's Word touches every facet of living. If we are really serious about discovering and doing the will of God, then we will get serious about reprogramming our minds with God's Word and facing every situation of life in the light of it. That kind of living will prepare us to discern God's plan for our lives as it unfolds before us step by step. "Then you will be able to test and approve what God's will is—his good, pleasing and perfect will."[17]

[14]Ephesians 5:25
[15]Romans 13:8 (KJV)
[16]2 Corinthians 9:7 (NIV)
[17]Romans 12:2 (NIV)

PART THREE
GOD'S PRIMARY PROVISION

CHAPTER 8
EQUIPPED FOR THE JOURNEY

Our discussion of God's will has brought us unavoidably to God's Word, the living and powerful tool which God uses to transform our lives and prepare us to carry out his perfect plan. There is no way we can overemphasize the Word in our discussion of divine guidance. The Word is God's primary provision for steering us on the path of his choosing. It is the basic equipment we need to follow his plan.

The writer to the Hebrews mentioned the matter of equipment relative to doing God's will. "Now the God of peace ... equip you in every good thing to do His will, working in us that which is pleasing in His sight, through Jesus Christ...."[1] Let's talk about that equipment.

We need equipment for almost anything we do in life. To repair a car engine we need a certain set of tools. To replace a broken screen door on the house we need a different set. To play tennis we need a certain kind of gear. To hike in the mountains we need another kind. And when we leave on vacation we usually take all the equipment we think we'll need while we're away. Just so, if we want to do God's will on our journey through life, we need to be properly outfitted and supplied. We need to take all the right equipment with us.

[1] Hebrews 13:20, 21 (NASB)

DIVINE OUTFITTERS, INC.

The Apostle Paul described the equipment we need when he said, "All Scripture is God-breathed and is useful for teaching, rebuking, correcting and training in righteousness, so that the man of God may be thoroughly equipped for every good work."[2] "Every good work" is nothing else than God's will for our lives (as we discovered from Ephesians 2:10). And what is it that thoroughly equips us to do these good works? *All Scripture!*

The Scripture does everything that needs to be done to help us live in God's will. It *teaches* us what is right. It *rebukes* us; that is, it shows us where we have gone wrong. It *corrects* us; that is, it brings us back to the right path when we stray. And it *trains* us; that is, it disciplines us in righteous living. The Scripture, in and of itself, thoroughly equips us, fully furnishes us, completely rigs us out to do the will of God.

The great Psalm extolling God's Word confirms this important principle. "Your word is a lamp to my feet and a light to my path."[3] We have discussed how a lamp lights the path in front of us, one step at a time. That lamp symbolizes God's Word, which is crucial to finding God's will. We cannot hope to find it apart from the Word. It is doubtful that God speaks in audible terms today. He has spoken in his Word, which contains all that he wants us to know for now. If we want to hear his voice and know his will, we need to go to his Word.

When a mathematician wants to find an unknown quantity, he uses known factors to do it. If X is unknown, but he does know that three times X equals six, then he can figure out that X equals two. The known factors help him find the unknown. If we want to discover what God wants us to do, we need all the absolute, invariable, known information that we can gather. The Word is the only known factor we have for sure, the only source of absolute truth. So we must fill our minds with that Word. The Psalmist wrote, "The entrance and unfolding of your words gives light; it gives under-

---

[2] 2 Timothy 3:16, 17 (NIV)
[3] Psalm 119:105 (Amp.)

standing—discernment and comprehension—to the simple."[4] The "simple" are those who are not fully enlightened, who are still in need of spiritual guidance to keep them from being led astray. That would include all of us, wouldn't it? And God's Word provides the guidance we need.

God's leading is always in accord with his Word. The more of the Word we know, the more sound and solid information we can bring to bear on the decisions we need to make. Obviously, God's Word does not tell us what to do in every specific situation. It does not say whom to marry, or what occupation to choose, or where to take the family for vacation this year. But it does give us a great deal of information that bears directly on all those questions, and on every other decision we will ever face.

It is when our hearts are tuned to the Word and our minds are filled with the Word, that we are best equipped to recognize God's guidance. It works like this: As we learn more of the Word, we grow to think as God thinks, we learn to see things from his perspective. Our attitudes, our opinions, our goals, our ideals, and our values become more like his. When we face major decisions we are able to evaluate them with the mind of Christ rather than with the mind of the flesh.[5] In many instances we will automatically know what God wants us to do, and doing what he desires will become our daily life style and normal habit pattern of living.

The Word of God is the indispensable key to the whole subject of divine guidance. Think back to what we have already learned. We saw that the Word has assured us that God has a plan for every detail of our lives, and that he wants to reveal it to us step by step. We saw that we get to know him and learn to trust him through the Word. We saw that our minds are renewed and our lives transformed by the Word, so that we can be prepared to discern and do his will. And now we learn that the directions themselves are found in the Word. G. Christian Weiss summed it up beautifully: "There can never be any guidance contrary to the Word; there will seldom be guidance apart from the Word. Divine guidance

---

[4] Psalm 119:130 (Amp.)
[5] Cf. 1 Corinthians 2:15, 16

must either come through, or in perfect harmony with, the written Word of God. Anything else is not divine guidance."[6]

INSTRUCTIONS FOR USE

But how does God guide through the Word? When we buy a new piece of equipment we usually need instructions for using it. Maybe we should have some instruction on how to use the divine equipment of the Word to find God's will for our lives.

There are four basic means by which God reveals his will to us through the Word. First, there are plain statements of his will—statements in which the phrase *will of God* or its equivalent is actually used in the passage. Second, there are positive and negative commands which tell us what God expects of us. Third, there are general principles that are relevant to our decisions. And finally, there may be strong impressions made on our minds as we read the Word.

We want to explore each of these in detail, but first we need to establish some guidelines. There is a right way and a wrong way to approach the Bible. The wrong way is to treat it as a magical fetish or superstitious charm, that is, to seek guidance from it as other people might seek it from a deck of cards or a pair of dice. Some Christians seem to think the Bible is some sort of sanctified soothsayer, a hallowed horoscope, or a holy Ouija board. When they have a question or a decision to which they have not been able to find an answer, in sheer desperation they close their eyes, empty their minds of any past knowledge of the Word, open the Bible at random, point to a text, and accept that fragment as divine guidance. Or maybe they use a casual dive into a Bible promise box to get an answer to their dilemma.

A great many Christians have been sadly disappointed at the results they have obtained by these methods. Some have gotten upset with God for letting them down, and their faith has been severely shaken. Although God did lead men by casting lots on some occasions before his Word was com-

---

[6]G. Christian Weiss, *The Perfect Will of God*, Moody Press, 1950, p. 80.

pleted, there is no indication that we should resort to such methods of chance today.

I am not denying that God has used isolated verses to bring comfort, encouragement, or guidance; nor that he has caused certain passages to come alive with decisive direction for the moment's need. He has done that for me, quite dramatically, in a number of critical circumstances in my life. But he did not give us his Word as an emergency consultation service. He gave it to us to reveal his mind and to remodel our lives. It takes time and study to learn and to change.

When a fellow receives a letter from his girl friend, he doesn't haphazardly pick several words out of the middle paragraph, pin all his hopes for the future on that one phrase, and disregard the rest of the letter. He wants to know what the whole letter says, and he understands that one phrase in relationship to its wider context. How can we stake a decision on a chance verse chosen like a sweepstakes ticket, or as Alan Redpath puts it, a "lucky dip" into a promise box?[7] We need to begin familiarizing ourselves with the whole of God's revelation.

In addition to this warning about the potential misuse of the Word, there are some positive guidelines to follow when we approach the Scriptures for direction. For one thing, we need to understand the words in their normal sense. Don't look for some deep, dark, hidden meaning. God has endeavored to reveal his truth to us plainly, not to obscure it from us. And while figurative language does occur, those figures of speech were used to teach literal truths. The words which the writers chose were generally intended to be understood in a normal sense.

Secondly, apply the accepted rules of grammar to what you read. Don't try to make it say what you want it to or what someone else has told you it says. Simply observe what the words actually say in their grammatical relationship to each other.

Thirdly, understand what you read in the context in which it appears. If the statement can be understood in more

[7] Alan Redpath, *Getting to Know the Will of God*, InterVarsity Press, 1954, p. 13.

than one way, choose the interpretation which is most consistent with the subject of the paragraph, and with the theme and purpose of the entire book in which it is found. We can probably find justification in the Bible for doing almost anything we want to do by lifting proof texts out of their context. That is not divine guidance.

In the fourth place, become familiar with the cultural and historical background of the original readers, and try to understand the passage as they would have understood it. Differing customs might have an effect on how we apply it to our situation. A good Bible dictionary, Bible encyclopedia, and books on Bible backgrounds will be helpful here.

Finally, be sure to recognize to whom the passage was written. While we gain benefit from every part of the Bible, it was not all written to be our rule of life as Christians in this age. For example, God commanded the Israelites to throw stones at a man who was found gathering sticks on Saturday.[8] Obviously that is not God's will for us today. While all Scripture is profitable, and while great principles of godly living are found throughout its pages, God's specific directions to us are found chiefly in the New Testament epistles.

LET'S GET STARTED

If we want to know God's will, and if the Bible is the supreme source of guidance, then we need to get started equipping ourselves for life's journey. As Jesus said, "Search the Scriptures."[9] Follow the example of the Bereans who "searched the Scriptures daily."[10] Take advantage of every opportunity to increase your knowledge of God's truth. When the church doors are open and the Word is being taught, be there.[11] Bring a notebook along with you and write down what God is saying to you personally through the exposition of the Word—what changes he wants you to make, how he wants you to live. Get involved in a home Bible class with a knowledgeable, spiritually minded teacher. Listen to tapes of reputable Bible teachers.

[8]Numbers 15:32–36
[9]John 5:39
[10]Acts 17:11
[11]Hebrews 10:25

Spend time in the Word privately every day. Read it slowly and thoughtfully, a paragraph at a time, pencil in hand. Look for information about the Lord himself—what he is like, how he thinks and feels, his purposes and priorities, his values and standards. Write them down. Ask yourself how the passage applies to your own life. Decide how God may want you to implement it in daily living. Write it down. You will be building a wealth of divine truth into your life that will help you evaluate your decisions from God's viewpoint.

Consider taking your vacation at a Bible conference or Christian camp where you not only find recreation but add to your understanding of the Word. Consider taking some Bible correspondence courses or some classes at a good Bible college. Whatever you plan to do with your life, it might be profitable to spend at least a year in a Bible college in order to establish a firm foundation in God's Word. Your grasp of the Scriptures will not come overnight. It will take time and discipline. But as you approach the Word with an open heart day after day, seeking the will of God, he promises to direct your path.

Alan Redpath tells how God used the Word to lead him out of the business world and into the ministry. First he wrote on a piece of paper all of his reasons for staying in business. Then he wrote all of his reasons for entering the ministry. He took that paper with him each morning as he met with God, desiring only to do what God directed. As he studied the Word day by day, God began to give him verses that answered his arguments for staying in business. It took more than a year, but eventually God eliminated every one of those arguments and left him with only the reasons for entering the ministry. He made his decision on the basis of God's priorities for his life as they were revealed through the Word. That is a valid use of the Word for finding the will of God.[12]

Isn't it time we got serious about studying God's Word? It's a big book, and none of us can be expected to master all of it in one lifetime; but that is no excuse for procrastination. What we learn today may help us in the decision we face tomorrow. Let's get started.

[12] Redpath, *op. cit.*, pp. 13, 14

CHAPTER 9
THIS IS THE WILL OF GOD

We as Christians have a distinct advantage over unbelievers when it comes to facing decisions. We not only know that our sovereign God has already planned the way that is best for us, but we have infallible information about his priorities that will help us follow his plan. We have the inspired Word of God. And God specifically mentions at least six things in his Word that are part of his will for our lives. He actually says, for all practical purposes, "This is my will for you." These six things have direct bearing on many of life's decisions. Let's look at them.

FIRST THINGS FIRST

God's first priority is to glorify himself through man's deliverance from the condemnation of sin. He wants everybody to be saved, and he says so several times. He says, for example, that he *"will* have all men to be saved, and to come unto the knowledge of the truth."[1] He says also that he is "not *willing* that any should perish but that all should come to repentance."[2] And he says that he "sent his Son into the world to seek and to save the lost."[3]

[1] 1 Timothy 2:4 (KJV)
[2] 2 Peter 3:9 (KJV); cf. also Matthew 18:14; John 6:39, 40
[3] Luke 19:10

This Is the Will of God

The first point in God's plan for your life, therefore, is that you be saved. You must start here if you ever hope to know the rest of God's will. Admit your sin. Agree that there is nothing you have ever done or can do that will commend you to an infinitely righteous God. Believe that Jesus Christ died in your place and for your sins. Then put your trust in him as your personal sin bearer and Savior. God will forgive your sins, assure you that heaven is your destiny, and set you on an exciting new road of peace and purpose here and now.

If God wants everybody to be saved, however, your own salvation is only the beginning. Now he wants to use you to bring others to a knowledge of the truth. "As the Father hath sent me, even so send I you," said the Lord Jesus.[4] Our purpose in the world as Christians is identical to Christ's—to be God's instruments to bring salvation to the lost. Every Christian is divinely commissioned to share the good news of salvation through Christ. And if that is first on God's priority list, it ought to be first on ours. Every decision we face should be evaluated in the light of how it affects our ability to share Christ with a lost world.

This priority of witnessing may affect your decision to marry. Do you see yourself as being a more effective witness for Jesus Christ married than single? If not, maybe God wants you to remain single. The priority of witnessing will also certainly affect your choice of a life vocation. In what line of work can you most capably be used to present Christ to the lost?

For some that could mean career Christian service. Many Christian young people have never seriously considered missionary work, or any other Christian service vocation, because they are not sure that they are called. So they have simply chosen another profession that appeals to them. That is hardly consistent. We should have a sense of divine call to whatever field we enter. We should have a settled assurance that it is the will of God. And *every* Christian young person should at least prayerfully think about the possibility of vocational Christian service.

Some may honestly see how their special skills or abil-

---

[4]John 20:21 (KJV)

ities, applied in some secular field, could put them in contact with people who would never be reached for Christ in any other way. And of course the ministry of the gospel by those in career Christian service requires the sacrificial support of others in secular employment. But whatever we choose for our life's work, this clear revelation of God's will concerning the salvation of the lost should be applied.

God's desire to bring the lost to Christ through us may also help a young person determine which college to attend. Secular campuses desperately need a Christian witness. Yet Christian schools have a role to fill in training Christian workers for service. Only God can tell you which is right for you, but this basic revelation of God's will should be considered when you make your choice.

The priority of witnessing may also help you decide which neighborhood to live in, or where to draw the fine line between luxuries and necessities as you establish your life style. Neighbors are prime subjects for evangelism, and the tremendous need for money in world evangelism should help us choose a modest level of living and put a high priority on giving.

Christians have a tendency to make decisions like these without considering the will of God. One young man refused to go to a Christian school to study God's Word because he wasn't sure it was God's will. Then he turned right around and spent his life savings on a fancy new sports car without even thinking about the will of God. That's not honest. A married couple declined a short-term missionary opportunity which they were qualified for and capable of handling, because they weren't sure it was God's will. Then they went out and bought a lovely home in a very affluent community and later admitted that they never thought about asking God his will in the matter. That's not honest. God wants us to discern his will in every issue of life by applying biblical principles fairly.

Each Christian may apply this first principle differently in different situations, but every Christian should consider it. As Bill Bright put it, "Every Christian should take spiritual inventory regularly by asking himself these questions: Is my time being invested in such a way that the largest possible number of people are being introduced to Christ? Are my talents being invested to the full to the end that the largest possible number of people are being introduced to Christ? Is my money, my treasure, being invested in such a way as to introduce the greatest number of people to Christ?"[5] How high is evangelism on your priority list?

THE CONTROL CENTER

"So then do not be foolish, but understand what the will of the Lord is. And do not get drunk with wine, for that is dissipation, but be filled with the Spirit."[6] Here is a second revelation of God's will.

Scholars seem to be agreed that the "and" which connects these two sentences provides a transition from general counsel to particular instances. In other words, getting drunk is a prime illustration of stupidity, and being filled with the Spirit is a prime illustration of God's will. God wants us to be Spirit-filled; that is his will for our lives. So we need to know what the Spirit-filled life is and how it relates to our decisions.

The biblical analogy between drunkenness and the filling of the Spirit is significant. It does not imply that we will act irrationally when we are filled with the Spirit, but it does introduce the concept of *control*. When a man is drunk he is not in control of himself. Something else controls him—alcohol. When a man is filled with the Spirit, someone else controls him—the Spirit of God.

But how can we put ourselves in his control? First, we must acknowledge the things which keep him from controlling us. In Scripture this is called confession of sin. We are to confess to God those things in our lives which have been contrary to his wishes—both attitudes and actions, things we have committed which we should not have done as well as things we have omitted which we should have done.[7]

Second, we must willingly yield ourselves to his control. This is the presentation of our bodies to him which we have

[5]Bill Bright, *Paul Brown Letter*, Campus Crusade for Christ, 1963.
[6]Ephesians 5:17, 18 (NASB)
[7]1 John 1:9

discussed before.[8] When we give up the right to run our own lives and put ourselves at his disposal, then we are in his control. But if the Spirit of God is to remain in control, we must cultivate an awareness of his presence and a dependence on his power.

This is accomplished largely by saturating our minds with his Word. Paul said to the Ephesians, "Be filled with the Spirit," and he said to the Colossians, "Let the word of Christ dwell in you richly."[9] When we study each context we find that basically the same things follow each command. Being filled with the Spirit and being filled with the Word are parallel to each other. As we meditate on God's Word, our hearts are drawn to Christ. Spiritual things take on greater importance for us and begin to fill our lives. We begin to act in conscious dependence on his power rather than our own. We are dominated or controlled by his Spirit just as he wants us to be, and when we are in that condition, he is free to lead us.

This was beautifully illustrated in the early days of our Lord Jesus' earthly ministry. "Jesus, full of the Holy Spirit, returned from the Jordan and was led by the Spirit in the desert."[10] He was filled with the Spirit and led by the Spirit. And if we want to be certain that the course we are considering is the leading of the Lord, we too must be certain that his Spirit is in control of our lives.

Just knowing that the Spirit-filled life is God's will for us, is going to have a definite effect on our everyday decisions. "Where shall we go on our date tonight?" Let's eliminate from consideration all those possibilities that will detract from our thoughts of Christ and weaken the Spirit's domination of our lives. "Shall we send our children to public school or to a private Christian day school?" That is a complex decision and a number of biblical factors should be weighed such as the quality of spiritual training we are providing at home, the children's individual spiritual strength, the need for a witness in the public schools, our children's

[8]Romans 12:1
[9]Colossians 3:16 (KJV)
[10]Luke 4:1 (NIV)

ability or inability to provide such a witness, and what would be the best investment of our money. Some things may counterbalance others, so we need to establish an order of priority from a biblical perspective. But one important factor on our list of considerations will be the degree to which we believe the public schools will detract from our children's thoughts of Christ and weaken the Spirit's control of their lives.

100% PURE

"For this is the will of God, your sanctification; that is, that you abstain from sexual immorality."[11] It is God's will that we be holy. The word *sanctification* means holiness, consecration, dedication to God. In this verse the word clearly applies to the purity of our physical lives, that is, abstinence from sexual sins. The Word of God makes it clear that to have sexual relations outside the bond of marriage is impure, and Christians are to abstain from such practices. A fellow never needs to question whether or not God wants him to have sexual relations with his girl friend. God has already made his will known in that matter. He always desires purity.

Some young people are trying to decide whether a certain special member of the opposite sex could be God's choice for a life partner; yet when they are together they are much too free with each other's bodies. The temptations they arouse in each other are more than they can handle. I can assure them on the authority of God's Word that they are not meant for each other, at least not so long as they are involved with one another physically. The Bible says, "Flee fornication."[12] More than that, it says, "Flee also youthful lusts."[13] If someone has become a source of sexual temptation to you, then God's will for you is to run in the opposite direction as fast as your legs will carry you. Get away from that relationship. It is not part of God's plan for your life. God's plan is purity.

[11] 1 Thessalonians 4:3 (NASB)
[12] 1 Corinthians 6:18 (KJV)
[13] 2 Timothy 2:22 (KJV)

AN ATTITUDE OF GRATITUDE

"In everything give thanks; for this is God's will for you in Christ Jesus."[14] This is one statement of God's will that many Christians find difficult to accept. They know they should thank God for the good things that happen to them, but they cannot bring themselves to thank him for the problems. They are convinced that some circumstances give them a perfect right to grumble, gripe, and complain. They may try to justify themselves by insisting that this verse only requires thanking God *in* everything, but not *for* everything. "I'm still thankful for the good things God has done for me, even in this miserable situation," they claim.

Paul clarified that in the same context in which he taught us that it is God's will for us to be filled with the Spirit. In the verses that follow, he listed four descriptions of the Spirit-filled life, one of which is: "Giving thanks always for all things unto God...."[15] God wants us to be thankful *for* everything, not just *in* everything. I don't think Paul meant that we should go around shouting "Praise the Lord" when a precious loved one is taken from us in death. That can be phony. Yet we can be genuinely thankful in our hearts for tragedies such as that, knowing that they are part of God's perfect plan for our spiritual enrichment.

Whenever we face adverse circumstances we are prone to ask, "What does God want me to do?" By that we usually mean, "What can I do to get this burden off my back?" The teenager whose parents are being harsh and unreasonable wants to know what he should do. The man whose boss is taking unfair advantage of him wants to know what he should do. The woman whose husband pays very little attention to her longs for advice.

The first thing God wants each of them to do is to thank him genuinely and sincerely for the problem, and to thank him for another opportunity to grow spiritually and to learn more about his all-sufficient grace. That thankful spirit may be the very thing God will use to relieve the tension and make the situation more tolerable. Do you want to know

---

[14]1 Thessalonians 5:18 (NASB)
[15]Ephesians 5:20 (KJV)

God's will for your life? It is that you give thanks always, in every situation, for everything.

KEEPING IN LINE

"Submit yourselves for the Lord's sake to every authority instituted among men: whether to the king, as the supreme authority, or to governors, who are sent by him to punish those who do wrong and to commend those who do right. For it is God's will that by doing good you should silence the ignorant talk of foolish men."[16] It is God's will for us to submit ourselves to the laws of the land. This is one way he can shut the mouths of those who oppose the gospel.

We all toy at times with decisions that involve breaking the law. For example, suppose I am running late to a meeting at which I am to be the speaker and where I must minister the things of Christ. I know that the leaders of the meeting will be getting worried and many other people will be inconvenienced. Would I be justified in edging the speedometer up over the speed limit to make up some time? I doubt very much that the highway patrolman who stops me will look favorably on trusting the Lord Jesus as his personal Savior after I give him my excuse for breaking the law.

What can we do about poor laws? We can work to change them, but as long as they are on the books, God wants us to obey them. The only exception to that rule occurs when man's laws contradict the clearly revealed commands of God. At that point we ought to obey God rather than man, just as Peter and John did when the Jewish Sanhedrin told them to stop preaching in the name of Jesus.[17]

This God-willed submissiveness to authority reaches beyond our attitude toward government, however. Employees are exhorted to be submissive to their employers.[18] Wives are encouraged to be submissive to their husbands.[19] Believers generally are asked to submit to the spiritual leaders of their local churches.[20] In fact, all of us are to develop a submissive

---

[16] 1 Peter 2:13-15 (NIV)
[17] Acts 4:18-20; 5:28, 29
[18] Ephesians 6:5, 6; 1 Peter 2:18
[19] Ephesians 5:22; 1 Peter 3:1
[20] Hebrews 13:17

spirit toward each other.[21] If you are wondering whether God wants you to stand up for your rights, or argue for your opinion, or insist on doing things your way, you have your answer. God wants you to be submissive.

ROCKS ON THE ROADWAY

This may come as a shock to some folks, but God wants us to suffer. Twice, Peter mentions suffering according to the will of God. In one place he says, "It is better, if it is God's will, to suffer for doing good than for doing evil."[22] In another place he says, "So then, those who suffer according to God's will should commit themselves to their faithful Creator and continue to do good."[23] Now these verses do not say precisely that it is God's will for *every* Christian to suffer, but they certainly imply that it could be. And if we do suffer, it ought to be for doing good rather than for sinful attitudes and actions.[24]

Two passages from Paul fit alongside these two from Peter. One passage says, "For unto you it is given in the behalf of Christ, not only to believe on him, but also to suffer for his sake."[25] The other passage says, "Yea, and all that will live godly in Christ Jesus shall suffer persecution."[26] The phrase "will of God" does not appear in these verses, but the truth is evident in the light of what Peter has said.

If we are living godly lives in this godless world, we are going to experience some kind of opposition for it. That is God's will, for he knows that it can draw us closer to him, make us appreciate him more, depend on him to a greater extent, and strengthen our spiritual lives. If we are breezing along through life without any static from the people of the world, one of two things is probably true—either we are not living godly lives, or else they cannot see it. If they do see it, some of them are going to strike out against us and cause us problems. God says so.

[21] Ephesians 5:21
[22] 1 Peter 3:17 (NIV)
[23] 1 Peter 4:19 (NIV)
[24] Cf. also 1 Peter 4:14–16
[25] Philippians 1:29 (KJV)
[26] 2 Timothy 3:12 (KJV)

I'm not talking about the kind of antagonism we can arouse by tactlessness, rudeness, or super-spiritual pomposity. I'm not talking about agitating people with our eccentricities in order to prove our spirituality. That only damages the cause of Christ. I am referring to living a godly life, graciously letting it be known that we belong to Christ, and then happily accepting whatever comes—anything from people snubbing us to doing us bodily harm.

We need to consider the certainty of suffering when we face the decisions of life, and not make our choices merely on the basis of what will help us avoid it. That the neighbors hate us for refusing to conspire with them to cheat the city is not a good reason for moving to a new neighborhood. That a nation is not particularly friendly to the gospel is not sufficient reason for crossing it off our list of potential places to serve the Lord. Jesus said, "In the world you will have trouble. But take heart! I have overcome the world."[27]

Here then are six clear declarations of God's will for our lives. God wants us to be saved, Spirit-filled, pure, thankful, submissive, and ready to suffer. Seek God's wisdom in applying them to the next decision you face.

[27]John 16:33 (NIV)

CHAPTER 10
CHARTING THE COURSE

The job of a navigator is to move his ship successfully from one point to another. His fundamental tool through the centuries has been the chart, a representation of the earth's surface with notations that help him carry out his task. With the assistance of a chart he can establish the course that will bring his ship to its destination.

The navigational chart for the Christian's life journey is the Word of God. That Word contains the facts he needs in order to establish the right course for his life. We have considered some of the Word's plain statements of God's will. Now we want to determine how the *commands* and *principles* of the Word relate to finding God's will.

THIS IS YOUR CAPTAIN SPEAKING

When God says to do something or not to do something, that is obviously his will for us whether the phrase "will of God" occurs in the passage or not. When he speaks clearly about a particular issue, we need no other guidance. We need only to obey. And there are hundreds of imperatives in the Bible that have direct application to our lives. We need to read the Scriptures with our minds open to these positive and negative commands.

Someone may object that occupying our minds with rules

will make us legalistic. True. But the biblical concept is not that we must occupy our minds with rules. Rather, it is that we occupy our minds with the Lord, and the more we get to know him and love him, the more we will want to please him. Since he tells us plainly what pleases him, it would be foolish to ignore it. He himself said, "If you love me, you will do what I command."[1]

We obviously cannot look at all his commands here but we can illustrate how some of them may affect our decisions. Then we can begin to look for other commands as we study the Word ourselves. Here are some examples.

People have asked me on occasion what they should do when another believer has wronged them. Often they have some ideas of their own, such as telling their pastor, or telling someone close to the offender who might get him to see the wrong he has done. But the human approach usually compounds the problem. Why settle for human reason when we have a divine directive? Jesus said clearly, "If your brother sins against you, go and show him his fault, just between the two of you. If he listens to you, you have won your brother over."[2]

Did you notice with whom God says you are to speak about the problem? With the person who has offended you. Just you and him alone. Nobody else! To tell anyone else is to speak against the offender, and that violates another biblical command: "Do not speak against one another, brethren."[3] To tell someone else is also to give a poor report of the one who has offended us, and such reporting disregards the exhortation to think only about good reports.[4]

If we go to the offending brother in a meek and gentle spirit[5] and he responds to us favorably, the problem has been solved and harmony restored. If he refuses to respond to our efforts, then we can take one or two others along to witness our genuine effort at reconciliation and to witness his response.[6] If he refuses to listen to their encouragement, then

[1] John 14:15 (NIV); cf. also John 14:21; 15:10; 1 John 5:3; 2 John 6
[2] Matthew 18:15 (NIV)
[3] James 4:11 (NASB)
[4] Philippians 4:8
[5] Galatians 6:1
[6] Matthew 18:16

we can tell it to the church. If the church agrees that he has transgressed, but he still refuses to listen and to acknowledge his wrong, then Christ says he is to be treated as a gentile or a tax collector, which seems to mean that he is to be separated from fellowship until he is willing to work it out.[7] This divinely prescribed procedure will help eliminate gossip from the church, destroy factions and strife, and reduce hard feelings among Christians.

Here is another example. Women have told me about outrageous things their husbands have done to them, then have asked, "Don't you think I should divorce him?" The Bible has the answer to that question. "To the married I give this command (not I, but the Lord): A wife must not separate from her husband."[8]

To "separate from" means literally "to divide." That it refers here to divorce is clear from the next verse, which insists that she remain unmarried if she does separate. God hates divorce.[9] It is never his perfect will. He clearly commands that a wife is not to divorce her husband, and likewise, that a husband is not to divorce his wife.[10] God would always be pleased for a couple to stay together, to seek counsel, and to work unselfishly to make their marriage succeed.

Why then does Paul even mention the wife separating? (He says, "But if she does leave, let her remain unmarried, or else be reconciled to her husband."[11]) Paul mentions separation because he recognizes that some may disobey Christ's command for one reason or another. If they do, then it is God's will for them to remain unmarried or else to be reconciled to their former mates.

Paul makes no mention of fornication, which may be the Lord's one exception to this rule.[12] Nor does he say what to do if you are already divorced and your former mate has remarried, thus making reconciliation impossible. But he leaves no doubt about the right decision if you are presently

[7] Matthew 18:17
[8] 1 Corinthians 7:10 (NIV)
[9] Malachi 2:16
[10] 1 Corinthians 7:11
[11] 1 Corinthians 7:11 (NASB)
[12] Matthew 5:32; 19:9

married and your mate has not had extramarital sexual relations. Stay married! That is God's plan for you as you chart your future course.

Speaking of marriage, how can we overlook one of the clearest commands in the Bible about whom you should marry, or, more accurately, about whom you should not marry. "Be not unequally yoked together with unbelievers."[13] This injunction prohibits a believer from being matched together with an unbeliever. That yoking or matching may refer to a number of things, but it certainly includes marriage, the closest bond in all of life. It is never God's will for a Christian knowingly and willfully to marry an unbeliever. Paul reinforced this standard when he gave permission for widows to remarry, adding, ". . . only in the Lord."[14]

This principle should also help a fellow or girl decide whom to date and whom not to date. It could be spiritually profitable to take an unbeliever to church with the prayer that he or she might come to know Christ through the public ministry of the Word, but other dating may lead to an emotional involvement, tempting the believer to rationalize God's command concerning marriage and step outside his will.

On the positive side, there are many passages that help us know whom we *should* date and marry. As we read our Bibles, we find numerous qualities that a man or woman of God should possess. It might be wise to list them as we study the Word, and then evaluate our prospects by that standard rather than by human criteria.

I have been asked by counselees whether they should take a job that is open at the time, or go on welfare. The Bible has an unmistakable command relating to that decision too. "For even when we were with you, we gave you this rule: 'If a man will not work, he shall not eat.' "[15] If a job is offered and a person is able-bodied, he has a responsibility to work.

Some excuse themselves by claiming that the available jobs are not suitable to their particular skills, or that they are

[13] 2 Corinthians 6:14 (KJV)
[14] 1 Corinthians 7:39 (KJV)
[15] 2 Thessalonians 3:10 (NIV)

beneath their dignity, or that they do not pay as much as welfare pays. So they become freeloaders and eat off of other people's labors. But work is God's basic means for providing our needs. It is a necessary part of life, and those who avoid it usually become a problem to others around them. That's what happened in Thessalonica. "We hear that some among you are idle. They are not busy; they are busybodies. In the name of the Lord Jesus Christ, we command and urge such people to settle down and earn the bread they eat."[16]

And while we are on the subject of work, let's talk about changing jobs. That is a decision which almost everyone faces at some time or other during his life. The important question is, "Why do you want to change jobs?" Is it to provide for your children's education? Is it to enable you to give more money to the Lord's work? Or is it merely so you can buy some of the material goods you have always coveted?

The writer to the Hebrews gave us a command that might affect this decision. "Keep your lives free from the love of money and be content with what you have."[17] I am convinced that some people jump from job to job because of an underlying attitude of covetousness. They are always hoping that the next job is going to provide the big opportunity to get rich. But their irresponsibility and instability can hinder them from providing continuity and security for their families. In some instances it even deprives them of basic necessities of life. God tells us to be content. Not lethargic nor lazy, but content. True contentment encourages us to be faithful to our responsibilities, and faithfulness is rewarded by God.[18]

The subject of jobs may bring the thought of vacations to some minds. What should we do for our vacation this year? God has a precept which affects that decision too. "Therefore be careful how you walk, not as unwise men, but as wise, making the most of your time, because the days are evil."[19] Vacations should be restful and relaxing, but they should

---

[16] 2 Thessalonians 3:11, 12 (NIV)
[17] Hebrews 13:5 (NIV)
[18] Cf. Matthew 25:21, 23; 1 Corinthians 4:2
[19] Ephesians 5:15, 16 (NASB)

101 Charting the Course

also be meaningful and productive. There is no time to waste. The people of the world are lost and dying without Christ. The days we have left to win them are numbered.

Even fun-filled vacations should include time to build our spiritual strength and rejuvenate us for the work God has called us to do. And even on vacation we should be alert for every opportunity to share God's good news of salvation in Christ. There is no such thing as a vacation from God. Christians who try to take one usually find their spiritual lives woefully weakened.

These are only a few illustrations of how biblical commands can help you make right decisions. Look for other commands as you read the Word, then think through their implications for your life. They may dispel the clouds of confusion as you chart your future course.

JUST ON GENERAL PRINCIPLES

The general principles of Scripture are every bit as essential to determining God's will as the precise commands. Principles are simply statements of fact, but the facts may have direct bearing on how God wants us to live.

Let me illustrate first by talking about how we spend our money. A basic principle of Scripture is that God is the source of all wealth. Moses informed his people that it was God who gave them power to get wealth.[20] David agreed: "Riches and honor come from you [God] alone," he declared. "O Lord our God, all this material that we have gathered to build a temple for your holy name comes from you! It all belongs to you!"[21] Paul concurred when he said that God is the one who richly supplies everything we enjoy.[22]

If all wealth comes from God and it all belongs to him, then he has the right to tell us how to spend all of it, not just the small percentage we give back to his work. He even wants to help us make our purchases, to decide things such as which house or car or washing machine to buy. There is some truth to the adage, "You get what you pay for," but the

[20] Deuteronomy 8:18
[21] 1 Chronicles 29:12, 16 (TLB)
[22] 1 Timothy 6:17

102 God's Primary Provision

question we ought to ask when we are ready to buy is, "Do we really need all that we plan to get?" Some extra expenditures may increase the life and value of our investment, or the economy of its operation, but others are for sheer luxuries that squander God's resources.

Maybe we should make our purchases as though the Lord Jesus were standing right beside us telling us what he would need if he were doing the buying. Too often we operate under the false assumption that we need bigger and better things than people who make less money than we do. Why should we assume that making more money entitles us to a higher level of living? When the owner of all the wealth in the universe walked the face of the earth, he possessed practically nothing. God may be permitting us to earn more money so that we can invest more in world evangelization, not necessarily so that we can live more comfortably. Awareness of the principle of God's ownership of all things can help us get our needs and our wants sorted out according to his priorities.

One day a lady came to my office to ask me what she should do about her brother who had swindled her out of her share of the small family inheritance. A man asked Jesus that very same thing one day, and he established a principle that helped my friend know God's will in her dilemma. "Someone in the crowd said to him, 'Teacher, tell my brother to divide the inheritance with me.' Jesus replied 'Man, who appointed me a judge or an arbiter between you?' Then he said to them, 'Watch out! Be on your guard against all kinds of greed; a man's life does not consist in the abundance of his possessions.' "[23]

The guiding principle is simply this—there are more important things in life than the material goods that money can buy. Learning this principle well can bring us great freedom and peace. No amount of assets could have compensated that woman for the damage she would have done to her relationship with her brother had she sued him for a little of the family inheritance.

Some folks are trying to decide which church God wants

---

[23] Luke 12:13-15 (NIV)

them to join. Biblical principles can guide them here too. For instance, Paul called the church "the pillar and ground of the truth."[24] Since Jesus claimed that he was the truth[25] and that God's Word is truth,[26] a true New Testament church would be one which magnifies the Lord Jesus Christ and emphasizes the preaching and teaching of his Word. We can use this principle to evaluate any church we attend, and we would be ill-advised to lend our support to one which has deviated from this biblical pattern.

In an altogether different vein, a high school student was trying to decide whether or not God wanted him to go out for an organized sport. Are there principles in the Word for decisions like that? Listen to the Apostle Paul again: "For physical training is of some value, but godliness has value for all things, holding promise for both the present life and the life to come."[27] Benefits can be gained from athletics, but there are other things to be considered as well. How will the time spent in practice affect his time with the Lord? How will it influence his walk with God? When a person begins to put sports before God, then he departs from God's plan for his life. If he is honest in the application of the principle, God will guide him.

One of the big questions in the minds of many Christians concerns what we call doubtful things—practices which some Christians think are permissible, but other Christians think are sinful. Should we engage in them or not? A number of biblical principles can help us decide. What is it we are questioning? Will it lead a weaker Christian into sin?[28] Will it become my master?[29] Will it harm my body?[30] Will it build me up spiritually?[31] Will it glorify the Lord?[32] Can I do it with a clear conscience? The principle of Scripture is that "whatever is not from faith is sin."[33] In other

[24] 1 Timothy 3:15
[25] John 14:6
[26] John 17:17
[27] 1 Timothy 4:8 (NIV)
[28] Romans 14:21
[29] 1 Corinthians 6:12
[30] 1 Corinthians 6:19
[31] 1 Corinthians 10:23
[32] 1 Corinthians 10:31
[33] Romans 14:23 (NASB)

words, if I cannot do it as a redeemed child of God in the joy of my salvation, then it is sin, and it will surely hinder God's work in my life.

Let me mention one more quandary Christians sometimes face. Should we share our hurts, our struggles, and our weaknesses with other believers, or should we keep them to ourselves? Some of us feel that our reputation as Christians and our influence for Christ would be destroyed if anyone ever found out what we were really like on the inside. But the biblical principle establishing the church as the Body of Christ should help us see this issue from God's viewpoint. "The body is a unit though it is made up of many parts; and though all its parts are many, they form one body."[34] "If one part suffers, every part suffers with it."[35]

How can we feel with one who is hurting if we do not know where he hurts? How can we support him before God's throne of grace if we do not know where he needs support? How can we bear his burden with him if we do not know what his burden is?[36] I am not suggesting that we broadcast all of our faults for everyone to know. But the practical outworking of this principle might demand a greater openness with one another than most of us have. The honest admission of our shortcomings to our closest Christian friends will be an encouragement to them. They will know that they are not the only ones with weaknesses. It will likewise be a blessing to us as they pray for us, encourage us, and check with us periodically on our progress. The proper application of this principle stimulates spiritual growth.

This has been just a small sampling of how to find guidance through the Word. May it be a challenge to you to search the Scriptures personally for both the commands and the principles that will help you discern the will of God for your future course.

[34] 1 Corinthians 12:12 (NIV)
[35] 1 Corinthians 12:26 (NIV)
[36] Cf. Galatians 6:2

CHAPTER 11
BUT I FELT LED

Who of us at some time in our Christian lives has not had a strong impression to take some course of action, an inner compulsion we believed to be the leading of the Lord? At times in my own ministry I have felt compelled to call someone on the telephone or stop at someone's home, only to discover that the person in question needed to talk to me at that precise moment. Those impressions seemed to be more than coincidental.

That kind of an experience should not be unusual for the child of God. The Spirit of God does apply gentle pressure to the yielded spirit of a person, burdening his heart with specific needs and leading him by placing certain impressions on his mind.

But the inner guidance of God's Spirit cannot be divorced from an accurate understanding of God's Word. To try to separate the inner from the written is to open ourselves to a variety of dangers. We have been discussing the place of the Word in divine direction. We have seen some specific statements of God's will in the Word. We have examined ways in which positive and negative commands of the Word can help us determine God's wishes. We have noted how general principles in the Word cast light on our decisions. Now let's explore the relationship between the Word of God and the inner urging of the Spirit.

OUR INALIENABLE RIGHT

The child of God has a right to expect guidance from the Spirit of God, and that guidance can come by the direct communication of the Holy Spirit with the believer's spirit. Being led by the Spirit is one of the chief identifying characteristics of a true child of God. The Apostle Paul wrote, "For as many as are led by the Spirit of God, they are sons of God."[1] The leading referred to in this passage is primarily leading into a new kind of righteous living by putting to death the sinful practices of the old sin nature.[2] But whatever the objective of the Spirit's leading, the certainty of it is clearly established in this verse. And it is stated in a passage which clearly refers to the Spirit's personal witness directly with the Christian's spirit. The apostle goes on to say, "The Spirit Himself bears witness with our spirit that we are children of God."[3]

Few would deny that God can place thoughts in our minds, or even control our minds, if he so chooses. Since he controls the circumstances which invariably affect the way we think, and since he controls the mechanisms by which our minds function, he obviously can direct our thinking.

Solomon agreed. "The king's heart is like channels of water in the hand of the Lord; He turns it wherever He wishes."[4] The Lord Jesus made a promise to his disciples which bears out this principle also. The disciples would have no need for anxiety when accused by the authorities for their faith, because the Holy Spirit would teach them in that very hour what they should say.[5] In other words, he would put thoughts in their minds.

The Apostle John, in a prophetic vision, saw a dramatic example of this principle operating in the lives of unbelievers as well. Concerning ten kings who will someday join forces with a future world leader, he said, "For God will put a plan into their minds, a plan that will carry out his purposes."[6] If God can put his plan in the minds of unbelievers,

[1] Romans 8:14 (NASB)
[2] Cf. v.13
[3] Romans 8:16 (NASB)
[4] Proverbs 21:1 (NASB)
[5] Luke 12:12
[6] Revelation 17:17 (TLB)

he can certainly do it for Christians. We should have no problem accepting the fact that the Spirit of God can communicate his will directly to the mind of the believer.

WATCH HIM DO IT

Leaf through the pages of the book of Acts and observe the Spirit of God personally leading his servants. He spoke to a deacon named Philip and instructed him to approach a specific chariot where he found an Ethiopian eunuch open to the gospel message.[7] He spoke to the Apostle Peter and instructed him to accompany the three men who had come from Caesarea to get him.[8] Peter obeyed, and found a Roman centurion named Cornelius hungry for the truth of God. As he later rehearsed the story to his friends in Jerusalem, he said, "And the Spirit told me to go with them without misgivings."[9]

When a group of prophets and teachers in the church at Antioch fasted and prayed, "the Holy Spirit said, 'Set apart for me Barnabas and Saul for the work to which I have called them.' "[10] Later on, as Paul was doing that work, he attempted to go into Bithynia to preach the gospel, but the Holy Spirit spoke again and told him not to go.[11] As he returned from his final missionary journey, he told the elders from Ephesus that, although afflictions awaited him, the Spirit was constraining him to go to Jerusalem.[12]

The evidence is overwhelming. The Spirit of God communicated directly with those men. Some Bible students believe that he spoke in audible tones, but the possibility exists that he merely placed strong impressions in their minds. And guidance like that has not been limited to New Testament personalities. It can happen today.

Zac Poonen tells the story of an American preacher who was led by the Spirit to a logging camp which he found

[7] Acts 8:29
[8] Acts 10:19, 20
[9] Acts 11:12 (NASB)
[10] Acts 13:2 (NASB)
[11] Acts 16:7
[12] Acts 20:22, 23

deserted. He was so certain of divine guidance that he went into the empty dining hall and preached the gospel. Years later a man approached him in London and reminded him of the incident. He had been the cook at the camp and was the only man there that day. He had hidden outside a window, listened to the sermon, trusted Christ as his Savior, and had gone on to serve the Lord.[13]

G. Christian Weiss tells of a missionary in South America who received the distinct impression that he should take a trip into the jungle. At nightfall, after a long and weary trek, he arrived at a hut where he found an old Indian on his deathbed. "Where's the book?" the old man asked, explaining that on the previous night he had cried to God for help and had dreamed about a messenger bringing a book. He had been told in the dream to believe the message of the book and he would be saved. Needless to say, when the missionary brought out his Bible and shared the message of salvation, the old Indian trusted Christ. God had surely led him to that hut.[14] Illustrations like this abound. The Spirit of God can impress his will upon our minds.

THOSE OTHER VOICES

But here's the problem. Impressions come from other sources besides the Spirit of God. For one thing, we may have strong inclinations that stem solely from our own selfish desires. I remember a young mother who felt strongly led to get a job. That impression could have come from God, but it may also have originated in a selfish desire to get away from the tedious routine of housework and child care, and to add a little glamour to her life. She never questioned the source of the impression, however. She just proceeded to find work. Her doing so brought devastating results to her entire family. As she reflected on it, her excuse was, "But I felt led." By that statement she tried to relieve herself of the responsibility for her poor judgment. But God does not accept the blame for things like that. Not every impression comes from him.

[13]Zac Poonen, *Where Do I Go from Here, God?* Tyndale House, 1971, p. 46.
[14]G. Christian Weiss, *The Perfect Will of God*, Moody Press, 1950, p. 86.

I can remember a young man with a sizable family who felt led to quit his job and go into professional Christian service. He had no training for the ministry he wanted to enter, he was not particularly gifted to do the work he wanted to do, and there had been no opportunities offered him to serve. As I questioned him, it became obvious that his primary motive for seeking Christian service was not the call of God, but an unpleasant job situation from which he could see no other way out.

Our impressions may be affected not only by our desire to add a little sparkle to our lives or to escape a difficult situation, but also by things as simple as the amount of sleep we have had, the condition of our health, our degree of confidence and self-acceptance, the past experiences which we cannot erase from our consciousness, our subconscious fears, a sentimental bent, or emotional stress.

More devious than any of these, however, is the inclination to indulge our lustful desires. We can convince ourselves of almost anything in order to satisfy the flesh. James Dobson tells of the couple who felt led to have sexual relations before marriage because they loved each other so much. They said they had gotten down on their knees and prayed about it and had received the assurance from God that it was all right.[15] That is mere self-deception.

Impressions can also find their source in the influence of others—close friends in whom we have great confidence, magnetic personalities whom we think could never be wrong, or merely the prevailing opinion of the people around us. It may be the opinion of other Christians with whom we fellowship, be it right or wrong. Or it may be the opinion of the world which has invaded our minds through the media or through the unbelievers with whom we come in contact.

And then there is the most subtle influence of all—that of the great deceiver. Did you know that Satan can put impressions on the believer's mind? That may sound frightening, but it is true. Satan transforms himself into an angel of light,[16] that is, one who professes to give accurate informa-

---

[15] *James Dobson Talks About God's Will*, G/L Publications, 1975, p. 9.
[16] 2 Corinthians 11:14

tion and provide competent counsel. In reality he is the prince of darkness, and by his clever impersonation he seeks to gain an advantage over us.[17]

He did just that to a new believer named Ananias, by convincing him that it was acceptable to give part of his money to the Lord's work and yet imply that he was giving all of it. Listen to Peter as he put his finger on the root of the problem: "Ananias, why has Satan filled your heart to lie to the Holy Spirit, and to keep back some of the price of the land?"[18] The source of that foolish impression in Ananias' mind was the archenemy of God's people, the master liar and father of all lies, Satan himself.[19]

Satanic impressions may be quite striking, as with one girl who assured me that God was leading her to marry an unbeliever. She described in glowing detail the unusual, almost miraculous, circumstances that had brought them together. Such amazing events, she said, had to be of God. But Satan is even capable of performing miracles to convince us of his lies.[20] Satanic impressions can be extremely forceful, almost to the point of obsession.

The strength of an impression does not necessarily measure its validity. It is difficult for us to admit that our impressions have not come from God. We want to believe that God is doing something special for us. We want to tell our friends about the unusual guidance we have received. And our pride makes us all the more vulnerable to Satan's suggestions.

With so many possible sources for false impressions, it should be obvious to us that we cannot trust all the thoughts that come to us. To empty our minds of all distractions and take whatever comes into them as the will of God, as some have recommended, is an extremely dangerous practice. When the mind is blank, Satan is free to implant his suggestions. And there is nothing he would rather do than get us to listen unquestioningly to the impressions of our minds as though they represented the very voice of God. The Apostle John encourages us to test the spirits to see if they are from

---

[17] 2 Corinthians 2:11
[18] Acts 5:3 (NASB)
[19] Cf. John 8:44
[20] Cf. 2 Thessalonians 2:9

God.[21] Paul tells us to test everything and to hold only to what is good.[22] But how can we do that?

THE ACID TEST

There are a number of ways we can check out these inner urges, and we shall be exploring them in the remainder of our study. But the most important means is by the Word of God. Isaiah said it well when he warned the people of his day against listening to other voices: "If they speak not according to this word, it is because there is no light in them."[23] Every impression that comes from God is consistent with his Word. Not one will ever contradict his Word. God cannot contradict himself.

So measure your inclinations against the Word—its direct statements of God's will, its positive and negative commands, its general principles. The Spirit of God uses the Word of God to lead us, and the more of the Word we know, the more capable we shall become at testing the source of our impressions. Exposure to the Word will not only help us distinguish our true Shepherd's voice from those other voices, it will also help us recognize some of those selfish motives which inspire many of our impressions. The writer to the Hebrews called it "a discerner of the thoughts and intents of the heart."[24]

If the young mother had examined her biblical responsibility to her small children and let the Word of God illumine her motives, she probably would not have gone to work at that time. If the man who wanted to quit his job had seen his scriptural responsibility to provide for his family, he would not have left his job to seek Christian service at that time. If the couple who engaged in premarital sexual relations had submitted to the standard of God's Word, they would not have followed their foolish notions. If the girl who wanted to marry an unbeliever had listened to what God had to say, she would have known that he was not leading her into that marriage.

[21] 1 John 4:1
[22] 1 Thessalonians 5:21
[23] Isaiah 8:20 (KJV)
[24] Hebrews 4:12 (KJV)

But even after considering everything that the Word has to say on an issue, we may still be confused as to what to do. Where shall we turn then? There is yet another way that the Spirit of God can lead us through the Word, and that is by using the Word itself to plant the impressions upon our minds.

I am not referring to a statement leaping from the pages of Scripture and telling us exactly what to do. That has happened on occasion, but it has been the exception rather than the rule. I am referring to God laying certain things on our minds as we read the Word with an open heart and a yielded will. The major theme or emphasis of a passage may impress us with the things that matter most to God, or have direct pertinence to a decision we are facing.

As I sought the mind of God about a new opportunity for ministry open to me in Escondido, California, certain things kept coming to my mind such as God's blessing on the ministry in which I was already involved, a concern for its well-being should I leave, a fear of the unknown elements associated with the new opportunity, a distrust of my ability to handle the prospective new work, and some of the disadvantages of the new situation. But as I got alone with God for an extended period of time and read consecutively through the book of Isaiah, God seemed to be impressing new thoughts upon my mind which I could not escape, thoughts that were summarized best by this passage: "Do not call to mind the former things,/Or ponder things of the past./Behold, I will do something new,/Now it will spring forth;/Will you not be aware of it?/I will even make a roadway in the wilderness,/Rivers in the desert."[25] Although it was contrary to my wishes at the time, I took God at his word and made the move. And where God led me he has done some unusually wonderful new things in what has become the most fruitful ministry of my life.

God may never lead me in that precise way again, and he may never lead you exactly in that way. But if we want only God's will for our lives, whatever the personal sacrifice, and if we open his Word to look for what he has to say rather than for what we want to see, we can expect him to speak to us through it. He has promised that his Word will be a light to our path.

[25]Isaiah 43:18, 19 (NASB)

PART FOUR
OTHER PRACTICAL PRINCIPLES

CHAPTER 12
ASK GOD

The battleground for every decision we face is the mind. That is where we wrestle with the pros and cons, weigh the potential consequences of each alternative, and ultimately make our choices. The impressions which weigh the heaviest and linger the longest in the mind will usually determine the course of action we take. What goes on in the mind is crucial!

That is why we must be sure our minds are controlled by God's Spirit. Remember Paul's exhortation to the Ephesians? "Don't be unwise," or "Don't be without your minds." And in the very next verse he charges, "But be filled with the Spirit."[1] We cannot trust our impressions if our wills are not so yielded to the Holy Spirit that he dominates our minds. But when he is in control, we can expect our thoughts to be his thoughts.

Since the mind is the high command headquarters where all decisions will be made, it must be not only controlled by the Spirit, but also programmed with the Word. We have dealt with that principle extensively. As Paul put it, "Let the word of Christ dwell in you richly as you teach and counsel one another with all wisdom."[2]

But there is a third matter which vitally affects the mind

[1] Ephesians 5:17, 18
[2] Colossians 3:16 (NIV)

JUST ASK

The Apostle James said it beautifully: "If any of you lacks wisdom, he should ask God, who gives generously to all without finding fault, and it will be given to him."[3] Wisdom—that is the major commodity we need as we stand at an intersection in our lives and ponder which way to go. Wisdom from above—we get it by asking God for it.

The central theme in the context of this verse is the suffering in a believer's life.[4] James wrote his book to Jewish Christians who had been driven from their homes and scattered among the nations. At that very moment they were being persecuted for their faith, and that meant decisions for them to make. Trials almost always present us with decisions. Where shall we go? What shall we do? With whom shall we talk about this problem? How shall we find help? And along with those questions comes the nagging question of why God allowed the trial in the first place. Why does he let ungodly people get away with so much while his own people suffer so?

Where can we find wisdom to handle the pressure of perplexities like these? Ask God for it. It's just that simple. Ask God for it!

How can we know what to do when God takes a precious loved one away from us, or when we face a long and serious illness in the family, or when we lose our job, or when the car breaks down, or the baby gets sick, or the neighbors get huffy, or the money doesn't arrive on time? We ask God for wisdom. If we want to know his will, we need to ask him.

[3]James 1:5 (NIV)
[4]Cf. v.2

Ask God

While this verse in its context refers to trials, it establishes a broad and basic principle that relates to every decision in life—a principle found elsewhere in Scripture as well. Jesus said, "Ask and it will be given to you; seek and you will find; knock and the door will be opened to you."[5] Whether it is one of the major decisions of life like the choice of a vocation or a mate, or one of those less consequential issues like where to go for lunch or what to cook for dinner, we are invited to ask God for wisdom.

Jesus did. Follow him as he faces one of the most serious decisions of his life. There were multitudes who numbered themselves among his disciples, but he needed only twelve of them to be with him continuously and to receive the intensive training necessary to carry on in his absence. Whom would he choose? "And it was at this time that He went off to the mountain to pray, and He spent the whole night in prayer to God. And when day came, He called His disciples to Him; and chose twelve of them, whom He also named as apostles."[6] If Jesus needed that much time in his Father's presence when he faced a major decision, how much more do we.

Read the Psalms and listen to King David cry out to God for guidance. "Lord, lead me as you promised me you would."[7] "Show me the path where I should go, O Lord; point out the right road for me to walk. Lead me; teach me; for you are the God who gives me salvation. I have no hope except in you."[8] "Tell me what to do, O Lord, and make it plain because I am surrounded by waiting enemies."[9]

David must have recognized the dangers of barging ahead with his own plans without consulting the Lord. And no wonder. There had been a vivid object lesson of those dangers some years earlier in Israel's history, and David was probably familiar with the story. As Joshua led his people in the conquest of the land, the inhabitants of Gibeon tricked

---

[5] Matthew 7:7 (NIV)
[6] Luke 6:12, 13 (NASB)
[7] Psalm 5:8 (TLB)
[8] Psalm 25:4, 5 (TLB)
[9] Psalm 27:11 (TLB); cf. also Psalm 31:3; 43:3; 139:24; 143:10

them into making a covenant of peace. That treaty would bring grief for years to come, and the Scripture tells us how it happened: "So the men of Israel took some of their provisions, and did not ask for the counsel of the Lord."[10] We cannot afford to make that kind of mistake if we want our lives to count for Christ.

Paul Little told an interesting story from his undergraduate days as he sought the will of God for his life. He had been running around to meetings, talking to people, reading books, and looking for some magic formula that would reveal God's will with sudden and dramatic certainty. Then at an Urbana Convention one of the speakers asked, "How many of you who are concerned about the will of God have spent five minutes a day asking him to show you his will?" The truth hit him with tremendous force and set him to praying.[11]

Ask yourself that same question. Are you seeking the will of God in some matter? Would you be willing to spend at least five minutes every day talking to him about it? That may be the very thing he is waiting for.

Maybe you are facing a significant decision in your life right now. You've been frantically seeking direction from one source after another. You feel yourself getting anxious and apprehensive about it. Your worrisome attitude is not only hindering your communion with God, but it is also short-circuiting your ability to think clearly about your options. Why not heed the advice of the Apostle Paul? "Be anxious for nothing, but in everything by prayer and supplication with thanksgiving let your requests be made known to God. And the peace of God, which surpasses all comprehension, shall guard your hearts and your minds in Christ Jesus."[12] Talk to God about the decision. Share your thoughts and feelings with him. Thank him for his promise to guide you, and enjoy the peace of mind which he alone can give.

Since prayer is such an important element in knowing the will of God, we should also pray faithfully for one another as

---

[10]Joshua 9:14 (NASB); cf. 2 Samuel 21:1-9
[11]Paul E. Little, *Affirming the Will of God*, InterVarsity Press, 1971, p. 17.
[12]Philippians 4:6, 7 (NASB)

we face life's decisions. Such intercessory prayer is illustrated in Paul's relationship with the Colossians. When he heard how they had been growing in Christ, he wrote, "For this reason, since the day we heard about you, we have not stopped praying for you and asking God to fill you with the knowledge of his will through all spiritual wisdom and understanding."[13] And he assured them that his friend Epaphras had joined him in his request. "He is always wrestling in prayer for you, that you may stand firm in all the will of God, mature and fully assured."[14]

Guidance is a worthy matter for mutual intercession. We ought to follow the example of Paul and Epaphras by standing with one another before God's throne of grace as we seek his mind. Solicit the prayer support of your friends. And as you pray, remember also the decisions they face.

BUT WHY?

Maybe some are wondering why prayer is so important, since God has already promised to lead us. The only answer we need to offer is simply that he told us to pray. And godly people obey. But there are probably many reasons why he requires it. For one thing, prayer is an admission of need. God wants to be sure we understand how helpless we are in our own wisdom. As long as we neglect to ask him for guidance we are implying that we know what is best for our lives and that we can handle our decisions without his help. But our human reasoning powers alone are far from sufficient to grapple with the immense decisions that confront us through life.

Solomon made that clear when he established his basic prerequisites for divine guidance: "And do not lean on your own understanding," he warned.[15] On the other hand, when we ask God to lead us, we are acknowledging that we are incapable of successfully directing our own future and that we need his help. That is exactly where he wants us to be—fully aware that apart from him we can do nothing.[16]

[13]Colossians 1:9 (NIV)
[14]Colossians 4:12 (NIV)
[15]Proverbs 3:5 (NASB)
[16]cf. John 15:5

God may have another reason for asking us to pray as well. Prayer is the communion of our hearts with him, the time when our minds are fixed on him. What more opportune time could there be for him to put his thoughts in our minds than in the quiet, meditative moments we spend in his presence? Some Christians might find it difficult to hear the voice of God if he did try to speak to them. They're moving in the opposite direction. They seldom spend any time talking to him. They ignore him for days at a time. They live far away from his fellowship. But when we cultivate the consciousness of his presence, we become more sensitive to his gentle prompting in our spirits.

God may clarify his will for us while we are actually praying. Convictions begin to form, issues begin to crystalize, and the fog begins to lift as the will of God comes into clear focus. If we have listed the advantages and disadvantages of a particular alternative, or the reasons why we would like to go in a certain direction, God may rearrange our priorities or transform our desires even while we pray. While Peter's guidance to Cornelius' house came in the form of a vision rather than an impression upon his mind, it did come while he was in an attitude of prayer.[17] And there was no doubt that it came from God.

The impressions God puts in our minds through prayer are not impulsive and irresponsible notions that send us scurrying off in one direction today and back in another direction tomorrow. They are deep convictions that form in our souls as we commune with God. And if they are truly from him, they will become deeper and firmer as we continue to wait patiently upon him in prayer.

THE RIGHT WAY TO DO IT

God does attach one major condition to praying for his will, however, and we need to explore it. Right after the exhortation to ask God for wisdom, James adds this note: "But when he asks, he must believe and not doubt, because he who doubts is like a wave of the sea, blown and tossed by the

---

[17] Acts 10:9

wind. That man should not think he will receive anything from the Lord."[18] The necessary condition is faith. It was also Solomon's first condition for enjoying divine guidance—"Trust in the Lord with all your heart."[19]

One thing we need to believe is that God will surely answer our prayer and direct our path. The temptation to doubt may come if God delays, but it is interesting to note the tense James used in his exhortation to pray. He said literally, "Keep on asking."[20] God knows the best time to reveal his will, but he wants us to keep asking until that time comes. Christ's imperatives are likewise in the present tense: "Keep on asking; keep on seeking; keep on knocking."[21] We cannot give up because we do not receive an answer as quickly as we think we should. Faith requires persistence.

Then we must also believe that God is at work within us, changing our desires and fashioning them after his own. That may be difficult to believe. Most of us have learned to suspect our desires of being selfish and sinful. And with good reason. We know our own hearts. We've observed how many times we have acted out of selfish motivation. And we remember God's warning through Isaiah that our ways are usually not God's ways.[22] But that need not continue to be true, for "it is God who is at work in you, both to will and to work for His good pleasure."[23] We need to believe that God is exerting his power in our lives, helping us to want the same things he wants.

Have you yielded your will to him? Do you sincerely desire his will above all else? Well then, what do you want to do? Where are you mentally? What do you find yourself thinking about? That may be the very thing God wants for you. Believe it as you earnestly pray for his wisdom.

Of course, we may still be doubting the sincerity of our own surrender. Do we *really* want God's will more than our own? Did we *really* mean it when we yielded ourselves to

[18] James 1:6, 7 (NIV)
[19] Proverbs 3:5
[20] James 1:5
[21] Matthew 7:7
[22] Isaiah 55:8, 9
[23] Philippians 2:13 (NASB)

him? Make those doubts themselves a matter of prayer. Admit to God that you have certain likes and dislikes; tell him about your desires and your will. Then pray again what Jesus prayed in the garden, and mean it from your heart: "Nevertheless, not my will, but thine be done."[24] Then believe that he will put his desires in your heart. And when the settled assurance of God's will does come, don't let Satan destroy it with doubts. God said he would lead. Believe that he has, and joyfully do his will.

PRAYER AND FASTING

Frequently associated with prayer in the Scripture is the practice of fasting. Does fasting have anything to do with prayer for God's will? It did when the Spirit of God told the prophets and teachers at Antioch to separate Paul and Barnabas apart for missionary service. Those directions were given "while they were ministering to the Lord and fasting."[25]

Fasting also played a part in the revelation of God's will to Daniel. He had been studying the prophecy of Jeremiah, seeking to discover God's plan for the nation Israel, but he could not fully understand it. So he set his face to seek the Lord "by prayer and supplication, with fasting."[26] While he was still praying, God sent the angel Gabriel who said, "O Daniel, I have now come forth to give you insight with understanding."[27] The result of Daniel's prayer and fasting was the unique prophecy of Israel's seventy weeks, outlining the future of that nation for years to come.

Nowhere is the believer today commanded to fast, and it certainly earns us no merit from God. But when knowing the will of God is so urgent that we want to give ourselves totally to the Word and prayer without even taking time to eat, it shows that we are deeply serious about it. And God honors that degree of devotion.

Fasting also helps us keep our minds on the purpose be-

[24] Luke 22:42 (KJV)
[25] Acts 13:2 (NASB)
[26] Daniel 9:3
[27] Daniel 9:22 (NASB)

fore us. It does not do that by eliminating all thought of food. I can assure you of that from my own experience. When I have fasted, the sensations in my stomach made me think about eating. But every hunger pang reminded me also of why I was fasting—to ascertain the direction God wanted me to go. Thus it helped me keep my mind on that goal.

But more important still, fasting clears our minds to meditate freely on the things of Christ. The blood that is normally required to digest our food is available to sharpen our minds and increase the effectiveness of our thinking processes. If you want to apply your full mental faculties to communion with God when you face a crucial decision, fast and pray. It is no magic oracle that provides quick and easy answers. It is no substitute for preparation of heart or knowledge of God's Word. But the Spirit of God may use it to contribute to your understanding of his will.

CHAPTER 13
FLASHING LIGHTS AND CLANGING BELLS

The prize for the most popular method of attempting to discern divine direction among Christians today would probably go to the use of circumstances. I know many Christians who try to figure out what God may be telling them through the events around them or through the situations in their lives. No study of the will of God could be complete, then, without considering what the Scriptures say about circumstances.

THE HAND THAT RULES THE WORLD

The Bible teaches that God is sovereign. That means he is superior in position, supreme in power, and unlimited by any other. He does what he pleases. Isaiah said that his purposes will stand and that he will do all his pleasure.[1] David said that he rules over everything.[2] Paul said that he works all things after the counsel of his own will.[3] That's sovereignty.

A sovereign God can obviously affect our circumstances if he so chooses, and the Scripture indicates that he does. He may actively cause things to happen that have direct bearing

---
[1] Isaiah 46:10
[2] Psalm 103:19
[3] Ephesians 1:11

on our lives. It may seem as though an event is purely accidental, or that other people have caused a particular situation, when all the time God is at work directing our paths.

For example, Joseph's jealous brothers sold him into Egyptian slavery. He may have thought at first that he had been the victim of their capricious actions, but years later he understood how it all happened. He said to his brothers, "And now do not be grieved or angry with yourselves, because you sold me here; for God sent me before you to preserve life."[4] God was directly responsible for that circumstance.

One day a Benjamite named Kish realized that his donkeys were missing, so he sent his son, Saul, to find them. Saul probably thought it was just one of those irritating events of daily living as he wandered unknowingly toward the place where the prophet Samuel was ministering. But the day before he arrived, God had told Samuel, "About this time tomorrow *I will send you* a man from the land of Benjamin, and you shall anoint him to be prince over My people Israel; and he shall deliver My people from the hand of the Philistines. For I have regarded My people, because their cry has come to Me."[5] God was superintending those circumstances.

In the early days of the church, fierce persecution broke out against believers in Jerusalem, driving them from their homes and scattering them throughout Judea and Samaria.[6] But everywhere they went they announced the good news of salvation through Christ,[7] and so began to fulfill the commission which Jesus had given shortly before he ascended into heaven.[8] We must conclude that God was directing those circumstances for the accomplishment of his own purposes.

And he can do the same for us. The circumstances in our lives may be more than coincidental. Suppose, for example, that a man has an excellent job opportunity in another city

---

[4]Genesis 45:5 (NASB)
[5]1 Samuel 9:16 (NASB)
[6]Acts 8:1
[7]Acts 8:4
[8]Acts 1:8

but feels rather negatively about the transfer. Then, quite unexpectedly, he meets a believer from that city who tells him about an excellent local church there with a particular need that he can fill perfectly. That experience could be God's way of opening his mind to the possibility of moving.

On the other hand, suppose his boss tells him they must close down his branch and it will be necessary for him to relocate in another city. He resigns himself to the unpleasant news without much thought. But the next day a friend calls to tell him about a job opening for which he is eminently qualified right in his own city. That could be God's way of opening his mind to the possibility of changing companies rather than relocating. God sometimes does things like that for us.

We often refer to God's leading through circumstances as consisting of open or closed doors. That is a biblical concept. John saw Jesus as the one who holds the key to every door of opportunity and service. "What he opens, no one can shut; and what he shuts, no one can open."[9] Paul spoke about open doors of ministry twice in his epistles.[10] Once he asked the Colossians to pray that God would open a door for his message.[11]

It is reasonable to assume that God will open doors for us to proceed in the direction he has determined. And it is obvious that he can close doors if he so chooses. He closed several for Paul and his companions. As we have seen, they tried to preach in Asia, but the Holy Spirit prohibited them. Then they tried to enter Bithynia, and the Holy Spirit would not permit that either.[12] The reason finally became evident. God was opening another door to a much wider ministry, and the gospel was about to penetrate the continent of Europe for the first time.

God can do similar things for you. By a rejection of an application he may show you which school to eliminate from consideration. By having a visa request granted or denied, he may show you what country he wants you to enter

[9]Revelation 3:7 (NIV)
[10]1 Corinthians 16:9; 2 Corinthians 2:12
[11]Colossians 4:3
[12]Acts 16:6, 7

for missionary service. When my wife was a teenager she thought God wanted her to be a missionary to China, but the Communist takeover in that country made it plain that he did not. That circumstance was one of the factors that helped her decide to marry me. Our sovereign God works in mysterious ways to perform his wonders. And circumstances often play a vital role.

BUT WHAT DO THEY MEAN?

Having said all that, however, I must quickly point out that circumstances are an uncertain guide. While God is in control of every event in our lives, most events can be interpreted in different ways.

You may have heard the story of two new missionary appointees who were on board ship with all their belongings, ready to set sail for a mission field. Before the ship left the harbor, it caught fire and all their baggage and equipment were destroyed. One missionary interpreted it as God telling him to stay home and teach in a Bible college—an alternative he had considered before deciding on missionary service. The other interpreted it as a Satanic hindrance, and so raised additional money for new equipment and left for the field several months later.

Which one was right? Both were greatly used of God in the years that followed. Maybe both were right. But there had to be other factors involved in their respective decisions. The circumstance alone was not determinative, because it was subject to varying interpretations.

Many different issues can affect the way we view our circumstances. The pressures of the world, the desire for the material things we think we need, selfish preferences about climate or locale, subconscious compulsions, false pity, or any number of other things may make us prone to interpret the circumstances to suit ourselves, and then try to use them to prove we are following God's leading.

We must also reckon with the possibility that Satan could be manipulating the circumstances. God does allow Satan some latitude to do that. For instance, Paul believed God wanted him to visit the Thessalonians on several occasions, but he indicated by inspiration of the Holy Spirit that Satan hindered him.[13] Satan can evidently deter us from doing God's will. He may be responsible for some of the impediments on our pathway, and we may not know for some time whether a specific circumstance is a divine door-closing or a Satanic hindrance.

If God is leading, he will ultimately open all the doors and remove all the obstacles. Every circumstance must eventually fall into place when we are following his plan. We will not need to break doors down or walk over people to do his bidding. When we struggle to remove obstacles by the energy of the flesh, we can be certain that we are setting our own course rather than following God's. He wants us to remember patiently that he will clear the way before us in his own time if we walk on his pathway. If doors remain closed, God may want us either to change our course entirely, or to go as far as we can and then keep knocking gently and waiting patiently on him. The circumstances alone do not tell us clearly.

Sometimes the confusion comes from having too many open doors. If you have acceptances from three different schools, or you have three different job offers, you obviously cannot take all of them. And there is no guarantee that any one of them is necessarily God's will. Every open door cannot possibly be the will of God for our lives.

The same thing is true of needs—another kind of circumstance. Some have said that the need constitutes the call to a specific service. But there are many more needs than we can personally meet, needs of a vastly different nature in every part of the world. If each awareness of a need were the revelation of God's will, we might feel led to change direction every time a new need came to our attention, and that would result in hopeless confusion. We cannot do everything that needs to be done, and God doesn't expect us to. He may lead you by burdening your heart with a particular need, but he does not want you to dissipate your energy by trying to attend to every urgent circumstance that clamors for your time. His plan for each of us includes the proper use

[13] 1 Thessalonians 2:18

of every minute, and our obligation is to use our minutes as *he* directs, to do what *he* wants done, not always what others demand. To find out what his priorities are for us as individuals, we may need to get alone with him, away from the commotion and pressure of people and circumstances.

Some Christians feel that God's blessing or lack of it is a significant element in guidance. But being used of the Lord does not necessarily mean he wants us to stay where we are or to keep doing what we are doing indefinitely. It didn't for Philip. He was engaged in a successful evangelistic campaign in Samaria[14] when God told him to go down to the desert and deal with one Ethiopian eunuch.[15] Although God has called us to one kind of vocation or to one field of labor, he may not want us to remain in it for life. In Bible times he often moved people from one place to another and from one calling to another, and he often does the same today.

Conversely, the lack of apparent blessing or the unpleasantness of a task does not necessarily mean that God wants us to move on. Pastors often feel that God is leading them elsewhere when a few people begin to disagree with them. But even persecution did not move the apostles in the early years of the church.[16] While others fled from Jerusalem, the apostles stayed.[17] And some faithful servants of God since then have been led to labor tirelessly for many years against overwhelming odds without any evident fruit. This encouraging promise from God has sustained them: "Let us not become weary in doing good, for at the proper time we will reap a harvest if we do not give up."[18] And God has been faithful to his Word.

God's leading in one circumstance may not necessarily mean that he wants us to do the same thing in a similar circumstance, either. Moses assumed that because God told him the first time to strike the rock to get water for his people, it would be permissible for him to strike it again on a later occasion. But he failed to enter the promised land be-

[14]Acts 8:5-8
[15]Acts 8:26
[16]Cf. Acts 4:1-31; 5:17-42
[17]Acts 8:1
[18]Galatians 6:9 (NIV)

cause of his false assumption.[19] We need to seek the mind of the Lord in every situation of life and not take any circumstance for granted.

Circumstances alone will seldom determine conclusively what God wants us to do. They may open our minds to possibilities we have not considered. They may establish a general direction to pursue. They may eventually confirm a decision as being right or wrong. But every circumstance must be considered in the light of God's Word, in an attitude of prayer, with sensitivity to the inner witness of God's Spirit, and in full commitment to follow his plan rather than our own.

God does not expect us to understand the meaning of every circumstance. "Man's goings are of the Lord; how can a man then understand his own way?"[20] Some of God's ways are unfathomable, unsearchable, "beyond tracing out."[21] While we should be alert to what he is endeavoring to do in our lives, we need not be constantly asking, "Why did this happen?" or "What is God trying to tell me by that?" We need simply to trust him.

SHOW ME

The mention of trust brings us to another facet of this subject—the seeking of signs from God. Some Christians are looking for God to lead them through supernatural phenomena—a bolt of lightning, a voice from heaven, a miraculous omen, a dream, or a vision. God did some spectacular things in Scripture. The children of Israel followed a cloud by day and fire by night.[22] The high priest got answers from God in some tangible manner by using the stones in his breastplate called the Urim and the Thummim.[23] Young Samuel heard a voice giving him instructions.[24] Joseph had a dream in which he was told to marry Mary.[25] God led the

[19]Exodus 17:6; cf. Numbers 20:7-12
[20]Proverbs 20:24 (KJV)
[21]Romans 11:33 (NIV)
[22]Exodus 13:21
[23]Exodus 28:30; Numbers 27:21
[24]1 Samuel 3:1-10
[25]Matthew 1:20

leaders of the early church through casting lots.[26] Saul of Tarsus saw a great light.[27] Peter had a vision.[28] Does God do things like that today?

Maybe the signs we seek are not quite that spectacular. We may merely be asking God for some small visible evidence of his leading. Abraham's servant did that when he sought a bride for Isaac. He stood by a well in Nahor and prayed. "Now may it be that the girl to whom I say, 'Please let down your jar so that I may drink,' and who answers, 'Drink, and I will water your camels also';—may she be the one whom Thou hast appointed for Thy servant Isaac; and by this I shall know that Thou hast shown lovingkindness to my master."[29]

Jonathan also did it when he pondered whether or not to attack the Philistines with only his armorbearer by his side. "If they say to us, 'Wait until we come to you'; then we will stand in our place, and not go up to them. But if they say, 'Come up to us,' then we will go up, for the Lord has given them into our hand; and this shall be the sign to us."[30] Should we seek verifications of God's will like that?

The story of Gideon's fleece is most often used to justify the seeking of signs. God told Gideon that Israel would be delivered from the oppression of the Midianites through his leadership, but he would not believe it. "Then Gideon said to God, 'If you are really going to use me to save Israel as you promised, prove it to me in this way: I'll put some wool on the threshing floor tonight, and if, in the morning, the fleece is wet and the ground is dry, I will know you are going to help me!'"[31] God condescended to grant Gideon his request, but he still would not believe. The next night he asked for the wool fleece to remain dry while the ground around it was wet.

And with that episode as a precedent, Christians are asking God for all sorts of signs. "Lord, if you want me to talk to those folks about Christ, you bring them to my house tonight." "Lord, if you want me to give that money to the

[26] Acts 1:23-26; cf. Proverbs 16:33
[27] Acts 9:3
[28] Acts 10:10, 11, 17
[29] Genesis 24:14 (NASB)
[30] 1 Samuel 14:9, 10 (NASB)
[31] Judges 6:36, 37 (TLB)

church, you give me an extra good week in my business." "Lord, if you want me to spend time in your presence, you wake me up early tomorrow morning." God can use events like these to help us understand his will, but the story of Gideon gives us no justification for demanding them.

May I remind you that Gideon's fleece had nothing to do with ascertaining God's will. He already knew what God wanted him to do, and he admitted it when he said, "If you are really going to use me to save Israel *as you promised* . . ."[32] His request for a sign was evidence that he did not believe God's Word. Jesus later said, "An evil and adulterous generation craves for a sign."[33] Christians are to walk by faith and not by sight,[34] and sign-seeking is in the realm of sight.

Scripture relates no instance of a believer seeking the will of God through signs after the day of Pentecost. Today we have the permanent indwelling of the Holy Spirit and the completed revelation of Scripture. We have no need for signs. To devise specific stipulations and to demand them of God is to reduce God to our mold, to make him after our own image, to create our own God. Let God be God! He must be free to deal with us as he pleases.

I'm afraid some Christians seek signs in an effort to relieve themselves of responsibility for their actions. "God didn't do what I asked him to do, so he must not have wanted me to . . ." But God does not always accommodate himself to our unbelief, our lack of spiritual discernment, or our carnal demands. He will not let us turn our personal relationship with him into a mechanical operation in which we punch buttons, pull levers, and get a readout of his will. He wants us to walk in fellowship with him, get to know him intimately, and then trust him implicitly to guide us by whatever means he chooses.

He may on occasion do something unusual or dramatic to confirm his will. That seems to happen most often to newer believers whose conscience is still underdeveloped, whose knowledge of the Word is still meager, and whose young and

---

[32] Cf. Judges 6:12, 14, 16, 23
[33] Matthew 12:39 (NASB)
[34] 2 Corinthians 5:7

tender faith needs to be strengthened. But in any case, we are not to be pleading for special signs nor sitting around waiting for them. We are to trust God and obey his Word.

YOU'RE DREAMING

Dreams are one particular kind of sign about which many Christians have special questions. After all, we do not necessarily want them nor do we usually ask for them. They just happen. Could they not be from God? In Scripture, the Spirit of God revealed his will frequently through dreams while the subject was asleep, and through visions in a waking state. Could he not use them today?

He certainly could. Few would deny that. And he has. Some have been led to the gospel through dreams. But dreams are hardly a consistently reliable guide. The experts tell us that dreams are the expression of thoughts from our subconscious minds, usually the result of something we have seen or learned through natural processes. Dr. James Dobson writes, "From a psychological point of view, dreams appear to have two basic purposes: they reflect wish fulfillment, giving expression to the things we long for; and secondly, they ventilate anxiety and the stresses we experience during waking hours. From a strictly physiological point of view, dreams also serve to keep us asleep when we are drifting toward consciousness."[35] If dreams reflect our own wishes or our own anxieties, we certainly will not want to accept them uncritically as God's guidance.

Even if the predictive elements in our dreams come true, that does not necessarily mean they are from God. There is still much to be learned about the mechanism of the mind. Even before the Spirit of God began his permanent indwelling ministry and before the Word of God was completed, God warned about trusting dreams alone. "Let these false prophets tell their dreams and let my true messengers faithfully proclaim my every word. There is a difference between chaff and wheat!"[36] Put your confidence in the wheat of God's Word, not the chaff of dreams.

[35]*Dr. James Dobson Talks About God's Will*, G/L Publication, 1975, p. 11.
[36]Jeremiah 23:28 (TLB)

CHAPTER 14
USE YOUR HEAD

The Word of God is primary in divine guidance. And the witness of the Spirit, clarified through prayer and confirmed through circumstances, will invariably contribute to our understanding of God's plan. But some other factors also affect the decisions we weigh. Some of these fit in the category of "the obvious." What is it you think God wants you to do? Ask yourself some self-evident questions about it.

DOES THIS MAKE SENSE?

I know that the most famous passage in all the Bible on God's direction forbids us from leaning on our own understanding.[1] But Solomon did not mean that we should shift our brain cells into neutral before we make a decision. That would be contrary to a great body of biblical truth. On a number of occasions, New Testament writers used the verb *sophroneo*, which means "to be of sound mind, to be reasonable, sensible." Peter used it when he said, "The end of all things is at hand; therefore be of sound judgment."[2] In other words, use good common sense.

Paul used the adjective form of the same word when he

---

[1] Proverbs 3:5, 6
[2] 1 Peter 4:7 (NASB)

said that elders should be "sensible,"[3] or literally, "of sound mind." He used the adverb form when he declared that the grace of God teaches us "to live sensibly."[4] We can be expected to live sensibly because "God did not give us a spirit of timidity . . . but . . . of power and of love and of calm and well-balanced mind."[5] That well-balanced mind is the human mind enlightened and sanctified by the Holy Spirit. We must not lean upon human wisdom alone, and that is the impact of what Solomon was saying. But when we are yielded to the Spirit of God, he helps us think clearly and sensibly, and that is exactly what we ought to do.

God gave us our brains, the apparatus we need for making sound judgments, and he doesn't want them standing idle. He expects us to use them. Certain decisions are right simply because they make good sense. For example, if you're trying to decide whether or not to go on a picnic, it would make sense to get a weather forecast and to stay home if rain is due. If you have to get up early for work tomorrow, it would make good sense to go to bed at a reasonable hour tonight, not stay up to watch a late show on television.

Suppose your child has a rare disease and there is only one place in the country where you can get proper treatment. It would make good sense to go there and get the help that is available. If a lack of money stands in your way, talk to the Lord about it and solicit the prayer support of other Christians.

God will remove every obstacle that prevents us from doing his will. He does the things we cannot do, but he expects us to use the good sense he has given us. When God delivered Peter from prison, the angel supernaturally removed the chains and led him past two guards, then miraculously opened an iron gate before him. But once they were out in the street, the angel departed and left Peter to use his head.[6] God isn't going to do for us what he has endowed us to do for ourselves.

He may want us to gather facts on which we can base a

---

[3] Titus 1:8 (NASB)
[4] Titus 2:12 (NASB)
[5] 2 Timothy 1:7 (Amp.)
[6] Acts 12:5-19

sound judgment, or list the advantages and disadvantages of the various alternatives. For instance, if you are trying to decide what college to attend, you will need to compile some data. How much money do you have available? Which colleges fit your budget? What are your major areas of interest? What schools offer strong programs in those fields? We must trust God to guide us, but we must also take the responsibility for making an intelligent choice on the basis of the information we have. Insist on good reasons for the decisions you make.

When we moved to California, my oldest son, who would have been a senior in high school at the time, was offered early admission to a college in Tennessee. Both his high school record and his college entrance exams had demonstrated his ability to handle the work in spite of his young age. It was a most attractive offer for him since it permitted him to remain in the general vicinity where he grew up and to avoid the inconvenience of entering a new high school for his senior year. But I was reluctant to let him go. I wanted him to be with our family during the first year of our new ministry.

I asked him to spend some time alone with the Lord and prayerfully compile a list of the reasons why he felt God wanted him to accept that college offer. About an hour and a half later he came to me with the list. It included the human reasons which I had suspected, but along with them were some wise, spiritually sound thoughts. Those thoughts, as well as the promise of financial help which came unexpectedly that very day, convinced me that he was being led of God to enter college, and we granted our permission. Subsequent events substantiated his decision as being the right one, but it was a decision based primarily on sound reasoning and common sense.

Remember, however, that human reason is fallible. We can never be sure that we have obtained all the relevant facts, nor that we are interpreting them correctly. Beside that, God may want us to do something totally opposed to unsanctified human reason. He asked Abraham to leave his home, his business, and his friends without any knowledge of where he was going. It made no sense, humanly speaking; yet it was the will of God.[7]

It makes no sense to unbelieving parents that their son should turn down the family business to enter some low-paying Christian profession. But it may be God's will. It makes no sense to some people for a brilliant linguist to spend a lifetime working with one small primitive tribe of jungle Indians. But it may be God's will. If decisions are made in accord with the principles of God's Word, they take precedence over the dictates of human wisdom. All common sense must be subject to the scrutiny of God's Word.

IS THIS WHAT I OUGHT TO DO?

The Scripture teaches that basic moral values are inscribed on the soul of every human being. Those values may differ from person to person or from culture to culture, but there is in every person a sense of "ought," called conscience, which evaluates his behavior and either accuses or defends him.[8] God can use that conscience to lead us.

It is true that a conscience can be seared or branded by the effects of sin.[9] That happens when we regularly ignore its voice and neglect to heed its warnings. A conscience may also become overly sensitive and restrictive, prohibiting things which God permits.[10] That is usually the result of excessive criticism during childhood. There is also the danger of a conscience being defiled, that is, common or unclean.[11] A lack of discipline through one's early years of life may distort his conscience so that it allows things which God forbids. Each person's conscience is conditioned by knowledge, experience, and training, so it too must always be measured by the Word of God.

But there is still that innate compulsion or restraint which must be reckoned with. "I ought to help that blind man cross

---

[7]Genesis 12:1
[8]Romans 2:14, 15
[9]1 Timothy 4:1, 2
[10]Romans 14:1, 2; 1 Corinthians 8:12
[11]Titus 1:15

the street." "I ought not to eat so much at the dinner table. My body doesn't need it." "I ought to be spending more time with my children." Prayerfully heed the voice of conscience. It may express the will of God.

Closely linked to conscience is the plain sense of duty. Certain things are obviously God's will simply because they are rightfully expected of us. As the Apostle James said, "Anyone, then, who knows the good he ought to do and doesn't do it, sins."[12] If you have an exam tomorrow for which you have not studied, you need not struggle over whether you should go out with the gang or hit the books. You have a moral obligation to the people who made it possible for you to attend school to do the best you can. You don't even need to pray about it. Just start studying.

According to a book by J. Sidlow Baxter, praying for "guidance" when duty is clear can lead to grave sins, deep delusions, and pathetic regrets.[13] Balaam was the classic example of that. God had told him he was not to go and curse Israel, but he just couldn't get his mind off that money. So we find him right back in God's presence asking again what he should do.[14] God finally let him go even though it was contrary to his will, but Balaam consequently lost both the money and his life. If you know what God wants you to do, do it! Apologize to that person you wronged. Share Christ with that friend whose heart is open. Fix that leaky faucet your wife has been after you about. Pay back that money you borrowed. You don't need to pray about it. It's your duty.

Doing our duty has another application as well. When you face a difficult choice and honestly cannot decide what to do, just faithfully perform the next thing that is expected of you as part of your daily responsibilities. Guidance may come and greater opportunities may open to you while you are carrying out those obligations.

In his parable of the talents, Jesus reminded us that faithfulness in the little things will open wider avenues of service. To those men who had faithfully invested their five talents and two talents as he wished them to, the master of

---

[12]James 4:17 (NIV)
[13]J. Sidlow Baxter, *Does God Still Guide?* Zondervan, 1968, p. 35.
[14]Numbers 22:19

the household said, "Well done, good and faithful servant! You have been faithful with a few things; I will put you in charge of many things. Come and share your master's happiness!"[15] The way to be used of God to our greatest capacity, and to enjoy the assurance that he will keep us in the center of his will, is to be steadfast and dependable in what he has given us to do. Keep doing what you are doing, and do it well until new guidance comes.

AM I QUALIFIED FOR THIS?

God never calls on us to do a job which he does not equip us to do. It is doubtful, for example, that he will call you to minister in music if you cannot carry a tune. He may actually lead you to the job he wants you to do through a careful evaluation of your special interests, gifts, abilities, education, or training. Each one of us is a unique combination of skills and personal characteristics, the sum total of all our past experiences, singularly fitted for the role God wants us to fill. We each have particular God-given potential, and we need to discover what it is.

We may want to find a counselor who can administer a vocational guidance inventory to see what our unique interests are. Then we should be willing to try different things as new opportunities arise. I am not referring to a person jumping from one thing to another in an irresponsible search for the "perfect" job. God is not honored when we try to avoid our routine responsibilities just because they are monotonous. I am talking about a prayerful consideration of any opportunity for service that is offered to us.

By attempting to do different things, we may discover where our greatest talents lie and where we can most effectively be used of God. But by all means do something! God's call comes to the active, not to the idle. As many others have pointed out, it is easier to steer a moving vehicle than a stationary one. Trace the history of God's dealings with men in his Word and you will find that he nearly always laid his hand on those who were already engaged in some kind of meaningful activity.

[15]Matthew 25:21, 23 (NIV)

But it is interesting to note that he did not always call them to the same kind of service in which they were involved at that moment. Some were called to new and different tasks for which they did not feel qualified. Moses argued with God about leading Israel out of Egyptian bondage. "Please, Lord, I have never been eloquent, . . . for I am slow of speech and slow of tongue."[16] Listen to God's answer: "Who has made man's mouth? Or who makes him dumb or deaf, or seeing or blind? Is it not I, the Lord? Now then go, and I, even I, will be with your mouth, and teach you what you are to say."[17] He can help us do what we do not feel capable of doing.

In the final analysis, it really doesn't matter a great deal what we can or cannot do. What matters most is what God wants us to do with our lives and how he wants us to minister to others. He can provide additional training if we need it, and he can impart new gifts and abilities if he thinks we need them. He can take what we are and transform us into whatever he wants us to be, if we are willing. We are not capable of accomplishing anything eternally profitable through our own gifts and abilities anyway. They must be energized and operated by his power. "Not that we are adequate in ourselves to consider anything as coming from ourselves, but our adequacy is from God."[18]

God may use our past training if he so chooses. But he may also lead us in a direction that seems totally foreign to our past training. Survey any seminary classroom and see the diverse backgrounds of the people preparing for Christian service. There may be accountants, chemists, engineers, athletes, doctors, salesmen, and a host of other professions represented. God is more interested in our present submission to him than in our past education or experience.

WHAT DO OTHERS THINK?

Someone has suggested that if you are the only one who thinks a particular course of action is right, you'd better stop

[16] Exodus 4:10 (NASB)
[17] Exodus 4:11, 12 (NASB)
[18] 2 Corinthians 3:5 (NASB)

and pray about it some more. That isn't to say that one person is always wrong when the majority disagrees with him. But it does reinforce the great truth of Christian community, that God has brought us together into one body so that we can minister to one another.

The book of Proverbs makes a strong case for seeking the counsel of others. "Where no counsel is, the people fall; but in the multitude of counselors there is safety."[19] "A fool thinks he needs no advice, but a wise man listens to others."[20] "Without consultation, plans are frustrated, but with many counselors they succeed."[21] "Get all the advice you can and be wise the rest of your life."[22]

New Testament writers agree. Paul exhorts us to *admonish* one another.[23] The word means literally "to put in the mind," therefore, "to instruct or to warn one another." The writer to the Hebrews said we are to *exhort* one another. That word means "to comfort, encourage or urge."[24]

Other people who are not involved in our situation may be able to look at it more objectively than we can. They may have wider experience than we have had, or they may be able to see things we have overlooked. They may have a greater grasp of the Scriptures or a deeper insight into human nature. So seek the advice of mature Christian friends—pastors, elders, teachers, and in the case of young people, youth sponsors, moms, and dads. God put certain people in places of responsibility to help you, and it would be foolish to disregard their advice.

And be careful not to make Ahab's mistake, seeking counsel only from those who will tell you what you want to hear. When trying to decide whether or not to go to battle with the Syrians, Jehoshaphat asked Ahab if there were a true prophet of the Lord whom they might consult other than just Ahab's favorite 400 "yes" men. That's when he admitted, "Well, there's one . . . but I hate him, for he never prophesies any-

---

[19]Proverbs 11:14 (KJV); cf. also Proverbs 24:6
[20]Proverbs 12:15 (TLB)
[21]Proverbs 15:22 (NASB)
[22]Proverbs 19:20 (TLB)
[23]Colossians 3:16
[24]Hebrews 10:25

thing good."[25] We may be tempted to avoid counselors who disagree with us, but if they are spiritually minded people who know the Word, we do well to hear them out.

Some folks avoid seeking counsel because they think it indicates weakness or immaturity, or possibly a lack of spirituality or intelligence. They want to prove that they can handle their problems by themselves without any help from anybody else. But that is basically pride. To admit that we have a problem which we cannot solve, and then to seek help, is far more mature and intelligent.

Just talking to someone else may help us clarify the issues in our own minds. But in addition to that, God may use the counselor to bring new insight to the situation or to point out some biblical truth that has direct bearing on our decision. God can also advise us through the writings of great saints from past years. Read how God dealt with them. It may help you understand how he is dealing with you.

That is not to say that the advice of others is infallible. Nobody knows everything, and everybody has areas of bias and subjectivity. Weigh all the advice you receive carefully in the light of God's Word. Do not become overly dependent on the counsel of others. Ultimately we are responsible for our own choices, and we must answer to God for what we decide to do.

In some instances we are obligated to take advice from others. I am referring to those who are in authority over us. God has established an order of authority in many realms of life. Regarding the local church, for instance, he says, "Obey your leaders and submit to their authority."[26] The New Testament identifies the rulers of the local church as elders.[27] God does not lead us to minister in the framework of the local church in any way that is contrary to the wishes of its elders. We are to be in submission to them. They are in a position to evaluate us and they may be able to recognize our limitations better than we can. On the contrary, if the elders want us to exercise our spiritual gifts in a particular kind of

[25] 1 Kings 22:8 (TLB)
[26] Hebrews 13:17 (NIV)
[27] Cf. Acts 20:17, 28; 1 Timothy 3:5; 5:17; 1 Peter 5:1-3

ministry, we should give it serious and prayerful consideration.

The same principle seems to apply to a missionary who has placed himself under the authority of a particular mission board. As long as he is part of that organization, he is responsible to do what his superiors ask him to do. He can reason with them graciously if he feels that they are making a mistake. And if they ask him to do something that compromises his biblical convictions, he may have to resign and find some other missionary organization with which he can agree. But as long as he is under their authority, he has an obligation to submit to them.

God has placed a wife under her husband's authority.[28] God's will for her is to be with him as his helper. A loving husband will consult her, consider her opinions, and act unselfishly for her best interest. But she will find her greatest joy and satisfaction in submitting to him.

When God led me to accept the pastorate in California, it was difficult for my wife to adjust to the idea at first. She had felt all along that we would not be moving, and when I shared with her the reasons I believed God was directing us to go, she was quiet and noncommittal. The next day, as she went about her regular duties, she was praying continuously in her heart, "Lord, show me your will."

Suddenly she realized that her prayer was different from what it had been previously. During the weeks prior to the decision she had been praying, "Lord, show Richard your will." At that moment it dawned on her that God had shown me his will, and that his will for her was to be with me. From that moment on we both had perfect peace about the move, and a beautiful harmony of spirit united us.

When a husband asks his wife to do something contrary to God's Word, she has the right to decline respectfully.[29] Otherwise, God wants her to believe that he will work through her husband to do what is best for her. It makes good sense to live as God has ordained.

[28]Ephesians 5:22, 24; Colossians 3:18; Titus 2:5; 1 Peter 3:1, 5
[29]Cf. Acts 5:29

CHAPTER 15
PEACE LIKE A RIVER

The people of God in Isaiah's day had become prosperous, proud, self-sufficient, and self-indulging. They professed to worship God, but they did it "neither truthfully nor rightfully."[1] Their lives were steeped in sin and their hearts were obstinate and rebellious.

Isaiah faithfully called them to repentance and warned them of their coming captivity in Babylon. Listen to him plead: "Thus says the Lord, your Redeemer, the Holy One of Israel: I am the Lord your God, who teaches you for your profit, who leads you in the way you should go. Oh, that you had listened to my commandments; then your peace would be like a river and your righteousness like the waves of the sea."[2]

In the prophet's 2,700 year-old message to Israel there is a great truth concerning the will of God for believers today. The lesson is simply that God wants to lead us, he makes his way known to us, and when we follow his direction we enjoy an inner quietness and assurance that has all the abundance, freshness, and persistence of a deep-flowing river.

In other words, the crowning confirmation that we are

---

[1] Isaiah 48:1 (Berk.)
[2] Isaiah 48:17, 18 (Berk.)

walking in the will of God is *peace*. We can never know true peace when we go our own way. As the prophet pointed out, "There is no peace, says the Lord, for the wicked."[3] But when we go God's way, there is a beautiful calm within.

STRIKE ONE!

The Apostle Paul taught much the same truth to the Colossian Christians hundreds of years later. He had been telling them how they ought to live, naming things they should put out of their lives and things they should incorporate into their lives. But there would be some occasions when they might not know what God wanted them to do. How were they to decide those matters? "Let the peace of Christ rule in your hearts," he says.[4] The word *rule* actually means "to act as an umpire, to arbitrate, to decide." Here Paul chose a technical term from the sports arena to help us determine the will of God. He said that an umpire called peace would make the final decision.

Can you imagine a world series baseball game without an umpire? Fifty thousand fans are in the stands, the players are on the field, and the first pitch streaks across the plate. The catcher says it's a strike. The pitcher and fielders agree. The batter says it's a ball. Everybody in the dugout takes the batter's side. The fans are divided and total pandemonium breaks loose. There is no way the game can go on with that kind of confusion. But when the umpire steps behind the plate and calls, "Strike!" the uncertainty is dispelled and the tumult is averted. Not everybody will like his call, and there may be a little arguing about it, but not for long, because the players want to stay in the game until its end.

Just so, God has provided an umpire to end the uncertainty, settle the disputes, and avoid the confusion in our lives. When we are pursuing the path of his choosing, an inner tranquility and serenity will tell us so. A quiet confidence and contentment will come over us. We will feel good

[3] Isaiah 48:22 (Berk.)
[4] Colossians 3:15 (NIV)

about the direction we are going. Our minds will be at ease. As Isaiah put it, there will be peace like a river.

But if, on the other hand, disturbing and disquieting thoughts begin to oppress us, it may be God's signal to go back and rethink our decision, back to the Word, and back to our knees in prayer. We may even have to go back to the examination room of the heart and check out the sincerity of our yieldedness.

Suppose, for instance, you are considering marriage, but there has been a great deal of bickering between the two of you lately. The man you plan to marry isn't treating you very tenderly and lovingly. Or the woman to whom you are engaged is constantly nagging you about silly little things. You're beginning to feel unsettled and restless about moving ahead with the wedding. God may simply want both of you to get some counsel, change some of your personality traits, and grow in his grace a little more before you marry. But those uneasy feelings could mean you have been going your own direction rather than God's, and to ignore them could bring years of unhappiness.

It is painful and embarrassing to break an engagement. Yet that pain is small in comparison with a life of misery with a person whom God never wanted you to marry in the first place. Most people have a few second thoughts before the ceremony. That's normal. But a deep, agitating uncertainty must not be overlooked. God may be trying to say something.

God used the umpire of peace to lead a pastor friend of mine to a new church. He had preached in that church while in that city on other business. Although he had no thought of changing pastorates nor any knowledge of what the people were up to, they voted overwhelmingly to call him to be their pastor. He and his wife prayed diligently over the decision and followed every principle of divine guidance they had learned, but still they were not sure what God wanted them to do. They were being used of the Lord greatly where they were, and had no desire to move. One morning he woke up and said to his wife, "God wouldn't make us do something we really don't want to do, would he?" She agreed that he wouldn't, and so that morning they decided together to remain in the pastorate they were then serving.

He went to his office, wrote a letter declining the offer, left the letter on his desk, and went to teach a class for which he was responsible in their Christian day school. But his mind was in a turmoil. He struggled for thoughts as he paced from one side of the classroom to another, but he could not teach. "Lord," he prayed silently, "I thought I was supposed to have peace when I came into an understanding of your will. Where is the peace?"

Finally, in utter distress, he dismissed his class (much to the students' glee), returned to his office, tore up the letter, and wrote a new one—a letter of resignation from his church. "Suddenly the sweetest awareness of Christ's peace swept over me," he said as he related the story to me. And God soon gave both him and his wife great joy as they anticipated their new ministry. The umpire of God's peace had made the final decision.

CAN WE TRUST OUR FEELINGS?

When I shared these thoughts with a group of college students, one young man protested, "Isn't that being led by our feelings? How can we be sure those feelings are from God?" That is a valid question and it deserves to be answered.

If the feeling of peace were our only source of guidance, finding God's will would be hopelessly subjective. But we are assuming that prior matters have already been attended to. First of all, we are properly prepared—we know the Guide; we have yielded our wills to him; and our lives are being transformed by his grace. Second, we are living in the Word, applying its eternal principles to every issue we face. Some people say they have peace when they are disobeying God's Word. But God never gives his peace about something contrary to his Word. A sense of peace must always be tested by the Word.

Third, we are cultivating a deepening relationship with the Lord through prayer, claiming direction from him. Fourth, with sanctified common sense we are prayerfully evaluating our circumstances, our responsibilities, our gifts and abilities, and the advice of others. If we have been faithful in these ways, we can be certain that it is God's peace which has settled in our souls rather than a false sense of well-being. He promised us that![5]

But is it not possible for something or someone other than God to disturb the peace he wants us to have, and so divert us from his plan for our lives? Yes. Even on occasions when I knew God's will, I have felt uneasy because I thought I might do a poor job and disgrace myself. My pride was destroying my peace. At other times, the prospect of great sacrifice, the anticipation of hard work, the fear of physical danger—any one of these might disturb us, and we may not even realize what is causing the absence of peace.

How can we count on peace to be a reliable umpire in cases like these? As we have seen before, the pathway is not always smooth in the center of God's will, and the thing that is threatening our peace may very well be one or more of those problems we are facing. So let's discuss further the matter of problems as they relate to God's will.

STORMY SEAS

How can we forget the afternoon Jesus made his disciples get into a boat to cross the Sea of Galilee while he went up into a mountain to pray?[6] "When evening came, he was there alone, but the boat was already a considerable distance from land, buffeted by the waves because the wind was against it."[7] Those disciples were out on that water by divine constraint. They were in the will of God, yet their lives were in danger. Contrary winds and stormy seas evidently do not prove that we are out of God's will. They may prod us to examine the reasons for the direction we are going, but not necessarily to alter it.

We can expect trials, hardships, sacrifices, and difficulties in the will of God. Don't shrink from them. They are part of his plan to bring us to maturity. In fact, when we receive them in the right spirit, they actually increase our desire to do God's will. Peter said, "He who has suffered in his body is done with sin. As a result, he does not live the rest of his

---

[5]Cf. Philippians 4:6, 7
[6]Matthew 14:22, 23
[7]Matthew 14:23, 24 (NIV)

earthly life for evil human desires, but rather for the will of God."[8] The Psalmist observed, "Many are the afflictions of the righteous."[9]

Biblical illustrations abound. For example, God sent Joseph to Egypt to languish in prison so that in due time he could preserve the nation Israel. Later, God led the children of Israel out of Egypt right into an awful wilderness so that he could take them home to Canaan. He sent Paul to Philippi where he was beaten and clamped in stocks, then later sent him to Jerusalem, warning him that bonds and afflictions awaited him there. And he sent his Son to the cross to suffer all the agony which our sin deserved.

We too will face hardships as we follow God's leading. One day as Jesus walked along the road, a man ran up to him and said, "I will follow you wherever you go." Jesus said to him, "Foxes have holes, birds have nests, but the Son of Man has no place to lay his head."[10] He gave us fair warning. To be his faithful disciples we must be willing to surrender the claim to everything we have.[11] And we might as well count the cost before we volunteer to do his will.[12]

But suppose we have counted the cost, given him all, sought his guidance, determined his will, and now we are joyfully walking in it, but then problems come and disrupt our peace. How do we handle that? We must go back to Solomon's first principle of divine guidance: "Trust in the Lord with all your heart."[13] If God's leading was clear when the sun was shining, don't doubt him when the storm clouds gather. Believe that the problems themselves are part of his plan. Keep your eyes on the Guide rather than on the obstacles, and move ahead by faith. Then trust will remove the uneasiness and restore the peace.

No amount of trust can reestablish peace in the heart of the Spirit-filled Christian if he accidentally steps off the path of God's choosing. That unrest is God's way of showing him

---

[8] 1 Peter 4:1, 2 (NIV)
[9] Psalm 34:19 (KJV)
[10] Luke 9:57, 58 (NIV)
[11] Cf. Luke 14:33
[12] Luke 14:28
[13] Proverbs 3:5 (NASB)

he has taken a wrong turn. It is also part of God's way of calling him back to the right road. But when we are walking in the center of God's will, with a firm trust in his sovereign and loving care, peace will reign in our hearts though the whole world crumble around us. Then to press on with confidence and perseverance in spite of suffering will bring great reward. "So do not throw away your confidence; it will be richly rewarded. You need to persevere so that when you have done the will of God, you will receive what he has promised."[14]

NO ANSWER

Another problem that frequently disturbs the peace of believers who are seeking guidance from God is a delay in getting answers. They want to do God's will; they have prepared their hearts, searched the Word, and sought the Lord, but still there is nothing. It's like trying to make an emergency telephone call, only to hear the phone ring and ring at the other end with no answer. We get nervous and fidgety when that happens. And we often get just as edgy when God doesn't answer our request for unmistakable leading. It happens often to college seniors who approach the end of the school year and still do not know what they will be doing after graduation. Instead of resting quietly in God's promise of guidance and intelligently investigating the opportunities that may be open to them, they panic and start wildly grasping at anything.

Most of us don't like to wait. We want answers now. We want things to work out for us right away. If it's any comfort to you, the Psalmist didn't like to wait either. "Lord, why are you standing aloof and far away? Why do you hide when I need you the most?"[15] "I plead with you to help me, Lord, for you are my Rock of safety. If you refuse to answer me, I might as well give up and die."[16] Job had trouble waiting too. "Oh, that I knew where to find God—that I could go to

---
[14]Hebrews 10:35, 36 (NIV)
[15]Psalm 10:1 (TLB)
[16]Psalm 28:1 (TLB)

his throne and talk with him there." "But I search in vain. I seek him here, I seek him there, and cannot find him."[17]

Our greatest mistakes in life are usually made because of our unwillingness to wait for God's timing. That's what happened to the nation Israel at Kadesh-Barnea. When God informed them that they would not be permitted to enter the promised land because of their unbelief, some of them got upset at the possibility of going back into the wilderness. The delay was more than they could handle. They thought that because they had admitted their sin they should be allowed to go right in, despite God's warning. But they lost their lives in the attempt.[18]

King Saul's refusal to wait also set him on a course that eventually destroyed him. God wanted him to bide his time until Samuel arrived to sacrifice a burnt offering in preparation for battle with the Philistines. But Saul couldn't wait. He intruded into the office of the priest, offered the sacrifice himself, and lost his kingdom as a result.[19]

We do it too. We make rash and foolish choices which we regret for years to come because we will not wait patiently for God to show us his will. Perhaps no major decision is more commonly made in haste than the decision to marry. Some fellows and girls seem to think that they may never have another chance if they let this one get away. So they move ahead into an unwise relationship that brings heartache and grief for a lifetime. Other people quit jobs for flimsy reasons, spend money frivolously and impetuously, sell a house and move to another city without any clear leading, or file for divorce without ever thinking through the consequences or seeing what God has to say about it in his Word. The Scripture says, "He who makes haste with his feet misses his way."[20] When we get into a big hurry, we are bound to make mistakes.

Why does God delay in giving us directions when we desire them so much? Isaiah makes one suggestion. "And

[17] Job 23:3, 8 (TLB)
[18] Numbers 14:39-45
[19] 1 Samuel 13:8-14
[20] Proverbs 19:2 (RSV)

therefore will the Lord wait, that he may be gracious unto you, and therefore will he be exalted, that he may have mercy upon you: for the Lord is a God of judgment: blessed are all they that wait for him."[21] The longer he waits and the more desperate our situation becomes, the more gracious and powerful is his deliverance and the more gloriously is he exalted. He waits so that he can demonstrate his mercy more dramatically and thereby magnify himself. Long delays are often followed by spectacular answers.

Periods of waiting can also be times of great spiritual growth, times when our faith is stretched and strengthened, when we get to know God more intimately. Baxter suggests that through the delay God may be trying to teach us something which is better even than the answer we are looking for.[22] His delays always have a purpose. Although we may not know what the purpose is, he asks us to trust him and wait.

Our impatience is usually due to unbelief, and we go back again to Isaiah's day to see it graphically illustrated. Judah was being threatened by the mighty Assyrians. The people were calling for some sort of treaty to placate them, or for an alliance with Egypt for protection against them. "Let's not just sit here and be destroyed; let's do something," was their attitude. Here was Isaiah's word from God: "Behold, I lay in Zion a foundation Stone, a tested Stone, a precious cornerstone, a sure foundation; he who believes will not be hurried."[23]

It was a prophecy of the coming Messiah, but it was also a reminder to those people that the God they worshiped in Zion (Jerusalem) was their sure foundation. If they would believe him, if they would put their trust in him, they would not need to rush out in fear and frustration and make some foolish treaty or alliance. Trust would be their only defense against a hasty decision. In our day, too, the only way we shall be able to wait patiently and peacefully for God to guide us is to trust him, to believe that his answer will come when we need it.

---

[21] Isaiah 30:18 (KJV)
[22] J. Sidlow Baxter, *Does God Still Guide?* Zondervan, 1968, p. 134.
[23] Isaiah 28:16 (Berk.)

We must not set time limits on God. He does not always work on our time schedule. We cannot hurry him. People may be yelling at us to do something decisive. Satan may be hurrying us to do something stupid that will ruin our lives. The flesh wants to take over immediately and do something brilliant and courageous that will prove its ability to handle any situation. But God is saying, "Just trust me, and wait."

David put it this way: "Wait on the Lord; be of good courage, and he shall strengthen thine heart. Wait, I say, on the Lord."[24] And it looks as though he took his own advice; for he was able to testify: "I waited patiently for God to help me; then he listened and heard my cry. He lifted me out of the pit of despair, out from the bog and the mire, and set my feet on a hard, firm path and steadied me as I walked along. He has given me a new song to sing, of praises to our God. Now many will hear of the glorious things he did for me, and stand in awe before the Lord, and put their trust in him."[25]

Has some decision been causing you to get impatient? Commit it to God. Tell him that you will trust him to guide you in his time. Ask him to help you wait patiently. And enjoy his perfect peace.

[24] Psalm 27:14 (KJV)
[25] Psalm 40:1-3 (TLB)

CHAPTER 16
RIGHT WHERE YOU ARE

Maybe you're thinking, "If only I had learned this years ago, my life could have been different. But I've wasted it now, and it's too late to change direction." I've heard that from folks who believe they've married the wrong person, or who failed to go to college when they had the opportunity, or who now think they've been pursuing the wrong career all these years, or who closed their spiritual ears once long ago when God called them into some form of Christian service. What happens when we miss the will of God?

We can miss it, you know. God made us with volition, and we are able to exercise that volition contrary to his wishes. We can thwart his perfect plan for our lives. We can go our own way.

OFF THE TRACK

The Bible frankly tells us about people who resisted God's will. In fact, the very first people we meet in its pages did that very thing. God created Adam and Eve to glorify himself through worship, fellowship, and obedient service. But they decided that their way would be more exciting and satisfying than his way, so they exercised their wills in opposition to him. Their descendants have been following their lead ever since.

People assert their own wills for many different reasons. Abraham took his wife's handmaid and had a son by her because *he thought it was the smart thing to do.* He wanted a son, and God had promised to give him one, so he thought God might like to fulfill his promise through Hagar. But he never thought to ask God about it.[1] It was human wisdom, fleshly reason. And we too can get sidetracked by listening to the wisdom of this world rather than to the voice of God. As one man confessed, "I thought God needed my money more than he needed me. So I went into business when he wanted me in the ministry, and now that my business has failed, God doesn't have either me or my money."

David committed adultery and then had the woman's husband killed. That pair of sins placed him far from the path of God's fellowship. And it all started when *he failed to fulfill his responsibilities.* He should have been with his armies, providing encouragement and leadership for them. Instead he was lounging around on his rooftop patio.[2] We too can get derailed from God's best when we shirk our God-given obligations. I'm thinking of a man who failed to show his wife the sympathetic tenderness that God requires of every Christian husband. Her negative responses to his inconsiderateness gave him all the justification he wanted for an escapade with another woman, and his sinful experience now has him on the shelf of uselessness.

Jonah found himself running in a direction opposite from God's, and it was nothing but *stubborn self-will* in his case. He didn't want to do what God had told him to do. God had instructed him to go to Nineveh and preach against its wickedness. Jonah said, "No way, God; I'm heading for Tarshish." And some of us have been running from God because we don't want to do what he has commanded us to do.

Peter denied his Lord three times, and but for Christ's intercessory prayers it would have wrecked the rest of his life. It seemed to be the result of a *human weakness*—his proud, presumptuous self-reliance. He had emphatically insisted, "Even if I have to die with you, I will never disown

---

[1] Genesis 16:1-4, 15
[2] 2 Samuel 11:1, 2

you."[3] But he did! Our weaknesses may be different from Peter's, but unless we recognize them and trust God for victory over them, they can get us off the track of his will.

Two other men who had contact with Jesus missed his plan for their lives because of *procrastination*. Jesus wanted them to follow him and be his disciples. One wanted to wait until his aged father died. The other wanted to go home and get everything in order, then come back when it was more convenient.[4] Some of us have put off doing God's will for so long that now we are convinced it is too late to follow his leading.

Whether it is due to human reason, or to nonfulfillment of our responsibilities, or to stubborn self-will, or to human weaknesses, or to procrastination, or to anything else, there are certain consequences for failing to do God's will.

PLEASURE—FOR A WHILE

Surprisingly enough, we may be quite happy about it at first. After all, Abraham did get his son, whom he named Ishmael. David had an exciting fling with a beautiful woman. Jonah got out of doing a disagreeable job. Peter got to see what they were doing with Jesus without exposing his identity. And those other two men got to go home where they wanted to be.

We may have gotten everything we were looking for back there at the time we considered God's way but willfully set out instead on our own course. We may have money, material possessions, status, acclaim, comfort, security, physical pleasures, marriage to that person who meant so much, or something else we considered important then. The writer to the Hebrews admitted that there are pleasures in sin for a season, and he was talking specifically about the glamorous things Moses gave up to do the will of God—the worldwide prominence of being in the royal family, and the fabulous wealth of Egypt.[5]

You may have it all. Everything may be going your way.

[3] Mark 14:31 (NIV)
[4] Luke 9:59–61
[5] Hebrews 11:24–26

And you may be quite pleased with yourself about it. "I did what I wanted to do and it turned out just fine. Why should I yield to God's will?" May I remind you that the game isn't over yet. Another biblical principle will certainly swing into operation, and it could begin at any time. It's the principle of sowing and reaping. "Do not be deceived: God cannot be mocked. A man reaps what he sows."[6]

For one thing, we will reap a harvest of guilt, remorse, and shame, just as Peter did when he went out and wept bitterly. Then we will reap the natural consequences of our sin. In Abraham's case, Sarah and her handmaid became insanely jealous of each other; turmoil invaded Abraham's happy home. Later, when Isaac was born to Sarah, rivalry broke out between the two sons—a rivalry that has continued to this day in the Arab-Israeli conflict. That's a rather long-lasting effect for one act of fleshly reason, isn't it? Some of David's children followed his poor example and brought heartache and grief to his family.

Insisting on our own way will eventually have a devastating effect on our lives. God has established basic principles for successful living. After we violate them we usually regret it. Mothers and fathers, for example, who neglect their children in order to enhance their careers or enlarge their net worth, eventually experience anguish of soul over those children. Husbands or wives who leave their mates for others often feel trapped in the tangled and complicated web they weave. These are some of the natural consequences of sin, and there may be no way to erase their marks from our lives.

Sometimes God intervenes directly with divine discipline as he did with Jonah when he sent a ferocious storm, fixed the sailors' election, fingered Jonah as the culprit responsible for their plight, then prepared a great fish to swallow him.

God can actually arrange a tragedy like that to stop us in our tracks and turn us in the right direction. And he does it because he loves us.[7] He knows that we can be totally happy and fulfilled only in the center of his will, and he wants us to

---

[6]Galatians 6:7 (NIV)
[7]Hebrews 12:6

have that fullness of joy. But the discipline itself is never an enjoyable experience. "No discipline seems pleasant at the time, but painful," the writer to the Hebrews reminded us.[8] Insisting on our own way always brings unpleasantness.

SOMETHING BEAUTIFUL

Maybe you're saying, "That's right where I am—out of the will of God, under his disciplinary hand, and feeling miserable about it. I don't want to keep on going this way any longer. What can I do?" For one thing, you need to be assured that your waywardness did not catch God by surprise. He knows everything! And he knew from eternity past that you would disobey him and go your own way, so he planned for it. He knew Adam and Eve would sin even before he made them, and before he ever created the world in which they would live he arranged a perfect plan to reclaim them and their sinful descendants for himself.[9] It was the best way to demonstrate the glory of his grace.

That's the kind of a God he is. He knew about our sinful self-will before he drew the blueprint for our lives. And now he is able to weave even our past sins and failures into a future that will glorify himself. As the Psalmist put it, "Surely the wrath of man shall praise thee."[10] Everything that happens is permitted by God. And he promises ultimately to use all of it to accomplish his own purposes. That's what Paul meant when he said that God works all things after the counsel of his own will.[11] "All things" must include our sin as well as everything else. God can make even our sins to praise him, as strange as that may seem.

Did you ever play the game in which one person scribbles a few lines on a piece of paper, then someone else has to draw a picture around it, using that meaningless scrawling as part of the picture? God is a master at that! He is the Great Adapter. Before we were ever born, he anticipated any mess we might make of our lives, and improvised an alternative

[8]Hebrews 12:11 (NIV)
[9]1 Peter 1:18–20
[10]Psalm 76:10 (KJV)
[11]Ephesians 1:11

plan in which our disobedience itself would ultimately serve a useful purpose.

Christ can take a shattered life and remake it into something more wonderful than it was before the wreckage. In fact, our serious mistakes and failures may be necessary to make us see how weak and sinful we are, and only when we recognize our weaknesses can we know Christ's power.[12]

So it makes no difference where you have been or where you are right now. God has a plan for you from this point on, and it is the very best plan possible. It may involve going back and doing what God wanted you to do in the first place, as it did with Jonah, who finally went to Nineveh, where God blessed his ministry.

But if it is impossible for you to go back and start again, God has a perfect alternative. I hesitate to call it "second best" as some have done, because right now it is the very best thing you can possibly do. You may have missed opportunities and joys that can never be recovered. But God has a plan for you to follow from this day forward that is absolutely perfect. It has to be, for it is his plan and he is perfect.

So don't look back with regrets. Preoccupation with previous mistakes will only contribute to future failures. Don't let the past deprive you of present blessing. Follow the example of the Apostle Paul: "Forgetting what is behind and straining toward what is ahead, I press on toward the goal to win the prize for which God has called me heavenward in Christ Jesus."[13]

But how can we forget all those wasted years? How can we forget the brokenness and strife which our self-will has left in its wake? There is only one possible way, and that is to confess our sins to God, forsake them fully, and then accept the gracious forgiveness which he offers. "If we confess our sins, he is faithful and just and will forgive us our sins and purify us from all unrighteousness."[14] He says that he removes our transgressions from us as far as the east is from

---

[12] 2 Corinthians 12:10
[13] Philippians 3:13, 14 (NIV)
[14] 1 John 1:9 (NIV)

the west.¹⁵ He says he remembers our sin no more.¹⁶ He says he casts them into the depths of the sea.¹⁷ If God is willing to forgive and forget, the least we can do is to accept his forgiveness and go on afresh.

That was what David did. His sin with Bathsheba made him miserable, "until," he says, "I finally admitted all my sins to you and stopped trying to hide them. I said to myself, 'I will confess them to the Lord.' And you forgave me! All my guilt is gone."¹⁸ And God was pleased to salvage his life and bless him. He did the same thing for Jonah, and for Peter, and he wants to do it for you. If you will acknowledge your sin, you can enjoy the sweet assurance of his forgiveness. If you will put yourself at his disposal, he will take you right where you are, make something beautiful of your life, and begin to use you for his glory. It's never too late to do the will of God.

WHY BOTHER!

Maybe some are thinking, "Well, if God can salvage my life at any point in time and use me for his glory from then on, I think I'll just keep going my own way awhile longer. He'll work out the problems I create and his grace will be magnified all the more." The Apostle Paul was afraid that some of us would think like that when we learned how gracious God is, so he said something about it in his letter to the Romans. "What shall we say, then? Shall we go on sinning so that grace may increase? By no means! We died to sin; how can we live in it any longer?"¹⁹

True believers share in the benefits of Christ's death, and he died to deliver them from the domination of their old self life. It is difficult to fathom a person who has been freed from the authority of his sinful nature, saying, "I'm going to sin more so God's grace will become more evident." Such an attitude casts doubts on his salvation. A desire to do God's will is one prime evidence of genuine salvation. When that

---

[15] Psalm 103:12
[16] Jeremiah 31:34
[17] Micah 7:19
[18] Psalm 32:5 (TLB)
[19] Romans 6:1, 2 (NIV)

desire is present, it brings assurance; when it is absent, it causes doubts. And one reason some Christians have so many doubts about their salvation is that they are doing their own will rather than God's.

Jesus said, "Not everyone who says to me, 'Lord, Lord,' will enter the kingdom of heaven, but only he who does the will of my Father who is in heaven."[20] On another occasion he affirmed that only those who do God's will are rightly related to him.[21] The Apostle John added, "The world and its desires pass away, but the man who does the will of God lives forever."[22] These verses do not say that doing God's will can secure for us eternal life, but they do indicate that the person who possesses eternal life will prove it by doing what God desires. One great benefit of following God's plan, then, is a blessed sense of assurance that we belong to him. "Therefore, brethren, be all the more diligent to make certain about His calling and choosing you."[23]

WINNERS AND LOSERS

Another powerful motive was suggested by the Apostle Paul: "For we must all appear before the judgment seat of Christ, that each one may receive what is due him for the things done while in the body, whether good or bad."[24] That word *appear* means "to be revealed." Someday every Christian is going to stand before Jesus Christ. There the quality of his life will be exposed. What comes out into the open at that time will be the basis for his reward. The person who has done the will of God by the power of the Holy Spirit and for the glory of the Lord shall receive a reward.[25] The person who has lived for selfish interests and poured his life into things of no eternal value shall suffer loss,[26] the loss of reward.

Some have said, "I don't really care about rewards. Just so

[20] Matthew 7:21 (NIV)
[21] Mark 3:35
[22] 1 John 2:17 (NIV)
[23] 2 Peter 1:10 (NASB)
[24] 2 Corinthians 5:10 (NIV)
[25] 1 Corinthians 3:14
[26] 1 Corinthians 3:15

I get there; that's all that matters to me." Do you realize what that means? Think about it for a moment. You do enjoy words of appreciation and commendation, don't you? It means a great deal to you when somebody says something kind, or does something thoughtful, or shares something nice unexpectedly, doesn't it? Being completely devoid of approval is more than most folks can bear. They long for some gracious word of praise. Living with no praise at all has led some into depression and despair.

Can you picture what it will be like before the judgment seat of Christ, when our precious Lord Jesus, in whom all of our joy and pleasure will be centered, will evaluate our lives? "Well done, good and faithful servant!" he will say to others around us. "Here is your reward." One after another, faithful servants of the Lord will be congratulated and honored. And now it's your turn. What will he say? The issue will not be primarily a matter of whether you went to church every Sunday or whether you gave a tenth of your income. It will be whether or not your will was fully yielded to Christ. Were you available to do whatever he asked? Was your life spent "doing the will of God from the heart"?[27]

John implied that there may be shame for some. "And now, little children, abide in him; that, when he shall appear, we may have confidence, and not be ashamed before him at his coming."[28] Shame! What a horrible thought—to stand before the Lord Jesus Christ with shame, the shame of an entire lifetime misused, misdirected, wasted. That fear should grip our hearts and compel us to do the will of God. That's what Paul was talking about when he said, "Therefore knowing the fear of the Lord, we persuade men."[29]

Paul takes us to the stadium again to cement this truth in our minds. "Do you not know that in a race all the runners run, but only one gets the prize? Run in such a way as to get the prize. Everyone who competes in the game goes into strict training. They do it to get a crown of laurel that will not last; but we do it to get a crown that will last forever."[30]

[27] Ephesians 6:6
[28] 1 John 2:28 (KJV)
[29] 2 Corinthians 5:11 (NASB)
[30] 1 Corinthians 9:24, 25 (NIV)

In the Olympic games, not every runner can win the race and receive a medal. There are only three winners in each event. But the Christian race is different. Everybody can win if he wants to. In fact, the only way to lose is to decide to lose by resisting the will of God. Why be a loser when you can win and receive a reward? The reward itself should not be our principal motive, but the Scripture still tells us about it and encourages us to run in such a way as to obtain it.

What a beautiful thing it would be to come to the sunset of our lives and to be able to say with Paul, "I have fought the good fight, I have finished the course, I have kept the faith; in the future there is laid up for me the crown of righteousness, which the Lord, the righteous Judge, will award to me on that day, and not only to me, but also to all who have loved His appearing."[31]

BEST OF ALL

But there is one motivation for doing God's will that is higher than all others. And again, it was Paul who mentioned it: "For Christ's love compels us, because we are convinced that one died for all, and therefore all died. And he died for all that those who live should no longer live for themselves, but for him who died for them and was raised again."[32] Christ's love! Above everything else, it is his love that seizes us and constrains us to live for him.

It was his love that drew him from the supreme glory he had in heaven to a sinful, self-centered world that despised and humiliated him. It was his love that led him to Calvary, where he bore God's fearful wrath against sin in our place. It was his love that caused him to offer us forgiveness and life when we deserved eternal condemnation. And when we grasp the immensity of that love, we shall live no longer for ourselves, but for him who truly loves us.

Doing the will of God is not a matter of gritting our teeth and toughing it out: "If I have to do it, I have to do it!" It is thinking about the one who gave everything to secure our

[31] 2 Timothy 4:7, 8 (NASB)
[32] 2 Corinthians 5:14, 15 (NIV)

eternal blessedness and then responding gratefully and joyfully to him. He loves you, just as you are, with all your sins and failures. He is ready to receive you when you offer your body to him as a living sacrifice. He is willing to transform you, empower you, and use you to accomplish his eternal purposes. Yield yourself to him. Then you will be able to say confidently with the Psalmist, "I delight to do thy will, O my God."[33]

[33]Psalm 40:8 (KJV)

FOOTNOTES

Chapter 5, footnote 8. From *Knowing God*, by J.I. Packer. © 1973 by J.I. Packer and used by permission of InterVarsity Press.

Chapter 8, footnote 6. From *The Perfect Will of God* by G. Christian Weiss. Copyright 1950. Moody Press, Moody Bible Institute of Chicago. Used by permission.

Chapter 8, footnote 7. From *Getting to Know the Will of God* by Alan Redpath. © 1954 by Inter-Varsity Christian Fellowship and used by permission of InterVarsity Press.

Chapter 9, footnote 5. Printed by permission. Copyright © Campus Crusade for Christ, Inc. (1963). All rights reserved.

Chapter 13, footnote 35. Reprinted from *Dr. James Dobson Talks About God's Will*. (Regal book). © Copyright 1975 Gospel Light Publications, Glendale, CA 91209. Used by permission.

Chapter 14, footnote 13. From *Does God Still Guide?* by J. Sidlow Baxter. Copyright © 1968 by J. Sidlow Baxter.

INDEX OF SCRIPTURE REFERENCES USED

GENESIS
12:1 p. 26, 137
13:14, 15 p. 26
16:1-4, 15 p. 157
24:7 p. 26
24:14 p. 130
24:27 p. 33
24:48 p. 26
28:20-22 p. 54
32:24-32 p. 55
45:5 p. 123

EXODUS
4:11, 12 p. 140
4:10 p. 140
13:21 p. 129
13:21, 22 p. 26
14:13 p. 44
17:6 p. 128
28:30 p. 129

NUMBERS
9:15-23 p. 31
13:33 p. 42
14:8, 9 p. 42
14:39-45 p. 153
15:32-36 p. 76
20:7-12 p. 128
22:12 p. 56
22:19 p. 56, 138
27:21 p. 129

DEUTERONOMY
8:18 p. 96
18:9-12 p. 12

JOSHUA
9:14 p. 115

JUDGES
6:12, 14, 16, 23 p. 131
6:36, 37 p. 130

1 SAMUEL
3:1-10 p. 129
9:16 p. 123
13:8-14 p. 154
14:9, 10 p. 130

2 SAMUEL
11:1, 2 p. 158
21:1-9 p. 115

1 KINGS
22:8 p. 142

1 CHRONICLES
29:12, 16 p. 96

JOB
23:3, 8 p. 153
31:4 p. 15

PSALMS
5:8 p. 114
10:1 p. 153
18:2 p. 45
23:1-3 p. 21
25:4, 5 p. 114
25:8, 9 p. 34
25:9 p. 53
25:10 p. 58
25:12 p. 53
27:1 p. 45
27:11 p. 114
27:14 p. 156
28:1 p. 153
31:3 p. 23, 114
32:5 p. 163
32:8 p. 23
32:9 p. 24, 49
34:19 p. 151
37:4 p. 58
37:23 p. 4, 29
40:1-3 p. 156
40:8 p. 168
43:3 p. 114
46:1 p. 45
46:10 p. 44
48:14 p. 24
73:24 p. 24
76:10 p. 13, 161
100:3 p. 20
103:12 p. 163

Index of Scripture References Used

103:19 p. 122
107:7, 8 p. 27
119:68 p. 46
119:105 p. 29, 72
119:130 p. 73
121:4 p. 18
121:8 p. 15
139:1 p. 9
139:1-5 p. 15
139:7-12 p. 45
139:13-15 p. 4
139:16 p. 4
139:23, 24 p. 63
139:24 p. 114
143:10 p. 114
147:5 p. 45

PROVERBS
3:5 p. 117, 118, 152
3:5, 6 p. 17, 40, 134
11:14 p. 141
12:15 p. 142
15:19 p. 25
15:22 p. 142
16:2 p. 62
16:9 p. 34
16:33 p. 129
16:25 p. 56
19:2 p. 154
19:20 p. 142
20:24 p. 129
21:1 p. 102
24:6 p. 141

ISAIAH
6:8, 9 p. 59
8:19 p. 12
8:20 p. 108
28:16 p. 155
30:18 p. 154
30:21 p. 34
42:16 p. 25
43:18, 19 p. 109
46:10 p. 45, 122
48:1 p. 146
48:17 p. 25
48:17, 18 p. 146
48:22 p. 146
49:1, 5 p. 5
55:8, 9 p. 119
58:11 p. 15

JEREMIAH
1:5 p. 6
1:6 p. 6
1:7-10 p. 6
10:23 p. 9
23:28 p. 133
29:11 p. 58
31:34 p. 163
32:17 p. 45
33:3 p. 23
42:3 p. 55
42:6 p. 55
43:2 p. 55
43:4 p. 55

LAMENTATIONS
3:23 p. 46

DANIEL
9:3 p. 120
9:22 p. 120

HOSEA
6:3 p. 48

MICAH
7:19 p. 163

MALACHI
2:16 p. 92

MATTHEW
1:20 p. 129
4:4 p. 47
5:28 p. 68
5:32 p. 93
7:7 p. 23, 114, 119
7:13 p. 14
7:21 p. 164
10:29-31 p. 15
12:39 p. 131
14:22, 23, 24 p. 150
18:14 p. 79
18:15 p. 91
18:16 p. 91
18:17 p. 92
19:9 p. 93
25:21, 23 p. 95, 139

MARK
3:35 p. 165
14:31 p. 158

LUKE
4:1 p. 83
6:12, 13 p. 114
9:57, 58 p. 151
9:59-61 p. 159
12:12 p. 102
12:13-15 p. 97
14:28 p. 151
14:33 p. 151
18:31 p. 7
19:10 p. 79
22:42 p. 56, 57, 119

JOHN
4:32 p. 7
4:34 p. 7, 58
5:17 p. 52
5:30 p. 7, 56
5:39, 40 p. 47
5:39 p. 77
6:38 p. 7
6:39, 40 p. 79
8:44 p. 106
9:2 p. 8
9:3 p. 8
10:27 p. 20, 46
14:6 p. 98
14:13 p. 23
14:15 p. 90
14:21 p. 90
15:5 p. 117
15:10 p. 90
16:33 p. 89
17:3 p. 42
17:17 p. 98
20:21 p. 80

ACTS
1:8 p. 123
1:23-26 p. 129
4:1-31 p. 128
4:18-20 p. 87
5:3 p. 106
5:17-42 p. 128
5:28, 29 p. 87
5:29 p. 145
8:1 p. 123, 128
8:4 p. 123
8:5-8 p. 127
8:26 p. 27, 127
8:29 p. 103
9:3 p. 130

Index of Scripture References Used

8:26-29 p. 32
9:30 p. 32
10:9 p. 118
10:10, 11, 17 p. 130
10:19, 20 p. 27, 103
11:12 p. 103
11:25, 26 p. 32
12:5-19 p. 135
13:1, 2 p. 27
13:2 p. 103, 120
14:27 p. 33
15:40-16:1 p. 33
16:6-8 p. 33
16:6, 7 p. 124
16:7 p. 103
16:9 p. 35
17:11 p. 77
18:9-11 p. 36, 103
20:17, 28 p. 143
20:22, 23 p. 36, 103
20:24 p. 2
22:10 p. 31
22:14 p. 27
22:14, 15 p. 2
22:15 p. 32
22:18 p. 32
22:21 p. 32
23:11 p. 36
28:16, 30, 32 p. 36

ROMANS
2:14, 15 p. 137
6:1, 2 p. 164
8:13 p. 102
8:14 p. 22, 102
8:16 p. 102
8:28 p. 16
8:32 p. 57
9:19 p. 13
11:33 p. 129
12:1 p. 83
12:1, 2 p. 49
12:2 p. 9, 58, 60, 69
13:8 p. 69
14:1, 2 p. 137
14:21 p. 98
14:23 p. 99

1 CORINTHIANS
2:15, 16 p. 73
3:14, 15 p. 165
4:2 p. 95
6:12 p. 99
6:18 p. 85
6:19 p. 99
7:10 p. 92
7:11 p. 92
7:39 p. 93
8:12 p. 137
10:23 p. 99
10:31 p. 99
9:24, 25 p. 167
12:12 p. 99
12:26 p. 99
16:9 p. 124

2 CORINTHIANS
2:11 p. 106
2:12 p. 124
3:5 p. 141
3:18 p. 64
5:7 p. 131
5:10 p. 165
5:11 p. 166
5:14, 15 p. 167
5:17 p. 3
6:14 p. 93
9:7 p. 69
11:14 p. 106
12:10 p. 162

GALATIANS
1:15, 16 p. 6
1:18, 19 p. 32
1:21-24 p. 32
5:20 p. 12
6:1 p. 91
6:2 p. 99
6:7 p. 160
6:9 p. 128

EPHESIANS
1:11 p. 12, 122, 162
2:3 p. 61
2:8, 9 p. 3
2:10 p. 3
4:28 p. 65
4:29 p. 68
5:8, 10 p. 65
5:15, 16 p. 95
5:17 p. 21
5:17, 18 p. 82, 112
5:20 p. 86
5:21 p. 87
5:22, 23 p. 144
5:25 p. 68
6:5, 6 p. 87
6:6 p. 166

PHILIPPIANS
1:29 p. 88
2:13 p. 58, 119
3:13, 14 p. 163
4:6, 7 p. 18, 116, 150
4:8 p. 91

COLOSSIANS
1:9 p. 23, 116
1:9, 10 p. 19
3:15 p. 147
3:16 p. 83, 112, 142
3:18 p. 144
4:3 p. 124
4:12 p. 23, 116

1 THESSALONIANS
2:18 p. 126
4:3 p. 84
5:18 p. 85
5:21 p. 107

2 THESSALONIANS
2:9 p. 107
3:10 p. 94
3:11, 12 p. 94

1 TIMOTHY
2:4 p. 14, 79
3:5 p. 143
3:15 p. 97
4:1, 2 p. 137
4:8 p. 98
5:8 p. 62
5:17 p. 143
6:17 p. 96

2 TIMOTHY
1:7 p. 135
2:22 p. 85
3:12 p. 88
3:16 p. 47
3:16, 17 p. 72
4:7 p. 2
4:7, 8 p. 167

Index of Scripture References Used

TITUS
1:8 p. 134
1:15 p. 138
2:5 p. 144
2:12 p. 134
3:5 p. 3

HEBREWS
4:12 p. 108
6:17 p. 13
10:7 p. 8
10:25 p. 77, 142
10:35, 36 p. 152
11:6 p. 40
11:24-26 p. 159
12:6 p. 161
12:11 p. 161
13:5 p. 95
13:17 p. 87, 143
13:20, 21 p. 71
13:21 p. 28

JAMES
1:2 p. 113
1:5 p. 113, 118
1:6, 7 p. 118
1:17 p. 57
4:11 p. 91
4:17 p. 52, 138

1 PETER
1:18-20 p. 161
2:2 p. 66
2:13-15 p. 86
2:18 p. 87
2:21 p. 57
3:1 p. 87
3:1, 5 p. 144
3:17 p. 88
4:1, 2 p. 151
4:7 p. 134
4:19 p. 88
4:14-16 p. 88
5:1-3 p. 143
5:7 p. 18

2 PETER
1:10 p. 165
3:9 p. 14, 79

1 JOHN
1:7 p. 65
1:9 p. 83, 163
2:17 p. 165
2:28 p. 166
4:1 p. 107
4:16 p. 45
5:3 p. 90

2 JOHN
6 p. 90

REVELATION
3:7 p. 124
13:8 p. 7
17:17 p. 103
20:15 p. 14